Qualitative

Lise Justesen & Nanna Mik-Meyer

Qualitative Research Methods in Organisation Studies

Hans Reitzels Forlag

Qualitative Research Methods in Organisation Studies
1st edition, 1st print run
Original title: *Kvalitative metoder i organisations- og ledelsesstudier*
Translated from Danish by Tam McTurk

© The authors and Hans Reitzel Forlag, 2012
Publishing editor: Martin Laurberg
Copy editor: Dorte Steiness
Cover: Ida Balslev-Olesen
Typographic design: Pamperin & Bech
Layout: Minon
Printed by Livonia Print
Printed in Latvia 2012
ISBN 978-87-412-5380-0

Hans Reitzels Forlag
Sjæleboderne 2
1122 Copenhagen K
Denmark

hansreitzel.dk

Contents

4. Focus groups

5. Participant observation

6. Documents

7. Qualitative research methods in organisation studies

Preface

Qualitative Research Methods in Organisation Studies is based on years of teaching courses at Copenhagen Business School in how different theoretical perspectives influence methodology in research projects. We both felt the acute need for a concise and highly practical, but nevertheless theoretically ambitious, textbook on qualitative methods, aimed specifically at students engaged in organisation studies.

"Highly practical" relates to our experience of the many relevant questions posed in classes and tutorials over the years that specifically focus on students' practical considerations when applying qualitative methods in their projects. "Theoretically ambitious" refers to the fact that, in order to answer specific questions of this type satisfactorily—e.g., how to formulate a question properly, choose the right interviewees or documents, or prepare thoroughly for data collection—students must reflect on the way in which a given theoretical perspective serves as the foundation for a study that incorporates qualitative methods and qualitative empirical material.

This methodology book aims to establish links between these two criteria. On a tangible level, this is done by placing the many practical questions about methods in direct relation to different theoretical perspectives, as well as by discussing the practical differences between working with a realist, a phenomenological or a constructivist perspective.

The book consists of seven chapters. Chapter One is a presentation of the three selected theoretical perspectives, focusing on the methodological implications for qualitative research. Chapter Two discusses a number of quality criteria that apply to qualitative studies, e.g., quality criteria that transcend the perspectives and quality criteria that apply generally. It also looks at quality criteria that relate more specifically to a realistic, a phenomenological and a constructivist perspective, respectively. Chapters Three to Six discuss four commonly applied methods used in qualitative studies—interviews, focus groups, participant observation and document analysis. These four chapters all relate to practical methodological questions in relation to the three perspectives presented. Each chapter includes a case study that illustrates the discussions. The book concludes with a summary chapter.

The aim is to stimulate methodological and theoretical reflection among students and improve the quality of projects in which they use qualitative methods. Along the way, the book contains references to a number of real-life examples of organisational research that, in various ways, use qualitative methods and analyses based on qualitative empirical material. These examples underline the idea that theoretical reflections are easier to communicate when exemplified. We hope that the book will be of practical use to the many students who work with qualitative studies. We would like to thank our colleagues at CBS, who over the years have contributed to several discussions about the relation between different theoretical perspectives and methodology issues. We would also like to thank Hans Reitzel Publishers and Martin Laurberg for all their help during the process of writing this book.

We hope you enjoy reading it.

Lise Justesen and Nanna Mik-Meyer,
Copenhagen, January 2012

CHAPTER 1

Theoretical perspectives and qualitative methodology

Introduction

Embarking upon a qualitative study raises a number of important issues about methodology. First of all, it is crucial that the student thinks about which of its many research traditions her study will reflect. In other words, which theoretical perspective will form the basis of her study? For example, is the objective to obtain exact knowledge of a phenomenon that is assumed to exist as an objective, autonomous entity? If that is the case, then the student's conceptual interest will be different than if she wanted to illustrate a phenomenon in all its complexity, i.e., where the assumption is that the phenomenon does not exist in the world as a distinct entity, but is (partly) created by the way we talk about it.

In terms of theory, the concept of the *perspective* can be used to encapsulate the various fundamental ontological and epistemological assumptions and conceptual interests upon which the student could base her work. It is important to emphasise that perspectives are not clearly delineated entities, nor is it possible to calculate their exact "number." For this reason, different books on theory and methodology do not always use the same designations. Precisely because theoretical perspectives are, to a certain extent, analytical constructs, in practice you will sometimes encounter research work that is difficult to place within a single, unambiguous perspective. A constructivist perspective and a phenomenological perspective can overlap, for example.

This book concentrates on three perspectives, which we call *realism*, *phenomenology* and *constructivism*. This was a deliberate choice, but by no means inevitable—we could have posited more perspectives, the boundaries between them could have been drawn up in a slightly different way, and we could have chosen slightly different names for them. There are several reasons why we chose to operate with these three particular perspectives throughout the book. The main reason is that they are often used in social research and, therefore, in research in what is referred to in this book as organisation studies.

Social researchers do not always explicitly state which perspective formed the basis of the research that underpins their books and articles. However, this does not mean that no perspective was applied during the research. The trained eye will often be able to work out and explain the implicit perspective that underlies a given study. However, it is a good idea for the student to think more explicitly about her choice of perspective, because it has—or, at any rate, ought to have—methodological consequences for the practical implementation of a study. If, for example, you are working on defining a problem and formulating an associated research question that will provide the basis for a study of processes within an organisation, and which will involve input from several parties, then developing clearly defined hypotheses for testing (verifying or falsifying) will not be the most obvious or best approach. In other words, the theoretical perspective has crucial consequences for the practical implementation of a study at all stages—deciding on the problem and formulating the research question, choosing a case study and interviewees, writing an interview guide, conducting a survey, other methods of selecting the style of argumentation, etc.—and especially for the analysis work.

The theoretical perspective is a designation for the fundamental understanding of the world and the basic view of knowledge upon which a theory is based. Some theories therefore take realism as their starting point. It might be said that they adopt a perspective that is based on a fundamental assumption that reality exists in a specific and, in principle, unambiguous manner "out there," *independently* of our knowledge of it. From this angle, the point of research is to capture the phenomena that interest us and to describe them as accurately, clearly and neutrally as possible. One objective may be, for example, to identify and explain cause-and-effect relationships between different phenomena, which in this context are often defined as *variable.*

Other theories use phenomenology as their starting point, and focus instead on subjective actions, especially with regard to the *meaning* that subjective actors attach to different actions. From this perspective, the researcher's objective is not to identify and explain causal relationships, but to interpret, understand and typify subjective universes of meaning.

A third option is constructivism, which assumes that our reality is continuously constructed through social processes. From this perspective, the job of the student is usually to attempt to capture the complexity that characterises the becoming of the phenomenon that interests her, and to describe as many facets as possible of that complexity and ambiguity.

Ontology and epistemology

The concepts of *ontology* and *epistemology* are often cited in relation to discussions of different research traditions. Ontology is the study of the nature of being. In brief, it refers to the question of what we perceive to be the nature of the world.

What "is" the nature of the objects of our analyses "in reality"? Do they exist as separate, distinct objects with inherent properties? Or is it the case that reality is ambiguous, "fluid" and socially constructed, and therefore not constant across different cultural, social and historical contexts? In other words, ontology is about how we view the part of the world that we have made the object of our study.

Epistemology is theory of knowledge. While ontology is about the part of reality that we make the object of our study, epistemology is concerned with our ability to attain *knowledge* of this subject area. How is knowledge possible? And what status does the knowledge have that we derive from our study? How sure can we be of our knowledge? Do subjectivity and context play a role in the knowledge process? If so, what role?

The realist perspective assumes that there is a single reality and that it exists in a certain form, independently of our language and knowledge. In this sense, it is objective. It might be said that realism operates on the basis of an essentialist and objectivist ontology. Both phenomenology and constructivism are critical of realism's ontological assumptions. Phenomenologists assume that there are multiple realities—or, as Schutz (1970: 252) puts it, "provinces of meaning". Constructivism could be said to go a step further. Like the phenomenologists, constructivists are critical of the notion that there is a single independent, unique reality, but also reject the idea that reality—whether singular or plural—has an inherent essence or a stable and coherent meaningfulness (Järvinen & Mik-Meyer, 2005). From this viewpoint, the object of study is never looked at independently of social processes and its specific context. Rather, it is constructed constantly, e.g., through the way that people talk about the world. Thus, constructivists maintain that constructed reality is both ambiguous and unstable.

One of the basic principles of the realist perspective is that to attain knowledge we must minimise subjective and contextual elements as far as possible. The ideal of knowledge is therefore objective in the sense that it is concerned with reflecting the object of the study as accurately as possible, namely the object *per se*. You might therefore say that ontology takes precedence over epistemology. Those working from the realist perspective acknowledge that it is an epistemological ideal, not attainable in a real-life research situation. However, the ideal itself implies a number of methodological endeavours that aim to minimise subjective influence. This is in contrast to both phenomenology and constructivism, which consider both context and subjectivity to be conditions of the study process that neither can nor should be ignored.

Quantitative and qualitative methodology

Many books on social research methodology operate with a distinction between *quantitative* and *qualitative* methods. The student who works empirically must decide whether her study will adopt one of these approaches or a combination of the two. As the term implies, quantitative methodology generates, in some sense or another, data that forms the basis for numerical analysis. In other words, quantitative methods generate material that consists of sub-elements that can be quantified and processed using various kinds of calculations, typically of a statistical nature.

The student who makes use of quantitative methods conducts, for example, large-scale questionnaire surveys that are processed statistically using software such as SPSS or other tools designed to analyse quantitative data. The student typically adopts these methods in order to provide a statistically based *description*—a snapshot of certain social conditions at a given moment—or an *explanation* of how certain factors are interrelated.

A quantitative study with a descriptive purpose may, for example, be one that shows how people would vote if there were a general election today, or what brand of mobile phone consumers prefer. In the latter example, the purpose will also often be partly to examine how preferences for certain brands relate to other variables, such as the consumers' age, gender, etc. A quantitative study therefore often identifies a general pattern within a certain area. In this type of study, it is typically the general aspect that is considered interesting and important. In other words, the results can be generalised in order to say something about other, similar situations.

Quantitative studies therefore presuppose that the phenomena we wish to study can be defined and delineated relatively unambiguously, and as such can be counted and presented in charts, tables, etc. This assumption means that many quantitative studies are often—implicitly or explicitly—based on a realist perspective.

Qualitative studies, on the other hand, use methods that are well suited to describe phenomena in context and, against that background, provide an interpretation that leads to a greater understanding of the phenomenon. Denzin and Lincoln (2000: 8) provide the following definition:

> "The word *qualitative* implies an emphasis on the qualities of entities and on processes and meanings that are not experimentally examined or measured (if measured at all) in terms of quantity, amount, intensity, or frequency."

The student adopts qualitative methodology when, for example, she opts to interview a small group of people personally and then interprets the interview material. Qualitative studies can, however, stem from a number of perspectives. They may arise out of realist, phenomenological or constructivist

Qualitative Research Methods in Organisation Studies

perspectives, that is perspectives that more (realism) or less (constructivism) assume that the phenomenon studied is delineated objectively "out there" in reality. However, qualitative studies will always, to a greater (constructivism) or lesser (realism) extent take into account the context that forms the framework for the phenomenon being studied. In studies where the student seeks both an explanation for particular interrelationships and an understanding of a phenomenon, it is not uncommon to combine quantitative and qualitative methods—for example a survey accompanied by individual interviews or focus groups.

In social research, the vast majority of quantitative studies are, to some extent, accompanied by qualitative studies, if only in the pilot phase, for example when the questionnaire is drawn up. Conversely, qualitative studies can stem from a quantitative questionnaire-based study that provides insight into more general patterns, and as such may indicate what the student should focus on in the qualitative study.

This book focuses on qualitative methodology and different forms of qualitative data—or, as it is often called in research informed by a phenomenological and constructivist perspective, "qualitative empirical material." Specifically, we will focus on interviews, focus groups, participant observation and document studies.

As mentioned, we have chosen in this chapter to present and discuss three regularly recurring perspectives from which many qualitative studies stem—a realist perspective, a phenomenological perspective and a constructivist perspective. In this chapter, our intention is not to discuss the subtle differences between the multiple variants within each perspective. Instead, we are trying to paint a general picture of the different perspectives in order to create a basis for a discussion of the practical and methodological consequences of the respective perspectives, regardless of which of the four methods mentioned above you choose to work with.

A realist perspective

Studies that adopt a realist perspective basically assume that there is an objective world "out there," i.e., independent of the researcher or the student who sets out to study certain aspects of it. As previously mentioned, realism therefore employs a realist ontology, whereby the assumption is that there is one single reality, the objects of which (in the broadest sense) have inherent, essential characteristics. The objective of the researcher working from a realist perspective is—as neutrally and objectively as possible—to describe and provide explanations for the phenomena and conditions that she is studying.

Some textbooks about research traditions, as applied to social research, divide realism into multiple sub-categories, for example "positivism," "critical rationalism" and "critical realism." Others talk about "neo-positivism," or "post-positivism." However, what they all have in common is that they operate with a realist ontology, in the sense that we have defined in this book. As such, reality is not presumed to be dependent on the social scientist that conducts the observations. She aims to describe the world objectively and considers this to be an important aspect of her research. Where these sub-categories differ from each other is partly in relation to how optimistic they are about their ability to generate knowledge that reflects reality in a neutral, accurate and unambiguous manner. However, as mentioned previously, objectivity, defined as the attainment of knowledge that reflects an objective reality, remains an *ideal* in the realist perspective. We can get close to descriptions that reflect reality itself, and we can refine our methods so we are able to test hypotheses, etc. Researchers working from a realist perspective, however, do not think that it is possible, in practice, to generate analyses that fully reflect the reality they wish to describe.

Realism in social research typically seeks to reveal the social structures in the world (and their underlying mechanisms) that govern human actions (May, 2001: 12). The assumption is that our knowledge of social reality interacts with the underlying structures in a way that influences our actions. The critical-realist-inspired researcher therefore has a dual focus: the actors involved (and their attitudes to and descriptions of the social world), and the underlying mechanisms and structures of which they are not necessarily conscious, but which nevertheless appear to regulate their actions. The researcher's task is therefore to reveal how the underlying mechanisms and structures affect the level that the researcher is able to register (Jespersen, 2004: 147). Metaphors that signal "depth," etc. are common in critical realism, as the assumption of this perspective is that human actions should be explained with reference to underlying conditions such as economic structures, power relationships, basic values in society, organisational principles, etc. Jespersen (2004: 149) shows, based on Lawson (1997), how a (critical) realistic project is typically structured:

Table 1. Structure of project based on critical realism

---

1) Formulating the research question →
2) The underlying object's ontology →
3) Epistemological discussion of possible theories (hypothesis formulation) →
4) Realist analysis method (based on "open" theories and empirical verification/falsification) →
5) Conditional conclusions →

(Adapted from Jespersen, 2004: 149)

The key point in Table 1 is that our object—that which is being studied—is assumed to be partially hidden (cf. the concept of "underlying"). However, it is important to emphasise that researchers are only able to observe the factual, empirical level, while realism's assumption is that what we see and hear is regulated by structural factors that are not readily accessible to us (or to the actors studied). The more our object is open to observation—the more we can see and hear—the more empirically based knowledge we are able to derive (Jespersen, 2004: 149). However, it is precisely because we cannot see and hear everything—because parts of reality remain hidden from us—that context also assumes major significance in the realist perspective. It is through studies of how context interacts with the object concerned that we are able to achieve knowledge of that object that is as precise and correct as possible.

This discussion and definition of the nature of reality is central to debates between realists and constructivists. According to Burr (1998: 23), discussions of what constitutes reality are based on the following three dimensions: 1) "truth" (what do we understand by the concept of true in relation to false?); 2) "materiality" (what do we understand by the concept of materiality in relation to illusion?); and 3) "essence" (what do we understand by the concept of essence in relation to construction?). These three concepts encapsulate the dimensions that form the basis upon which realists and constructivists discuss what is real and how this reality can be observed.

The point in this context is that realists and constructivists define reality differently, based on the three dimensions mentioned. Since analyses in social research must necessarily operate with a concept of the real world, whether it is conceptualised as a "reality" or a "construction," a logical consequence of the debate between realists and constructivists, therefore, is that it can be—and usually is—problematic to mix perspectives in the same study, as there is effectively no consensus about how to categorise and understand the (social) world under analysis.

A phenomenological perspective

Phenomenology stems from a specific branch of philosophy developed in the early 20th century by the German philosopher Edmund Husserl (1859–1938). Phenomenology has subsequently been further developed within philosophy itself, but elements of the social sciences, including sociology (Schutz, 1970), have also been strongly inspired by and adopted elements of phenomenology. In brief, phenomenology represents a break with the ideal of objectivity that is an integral part of the realist perspective. In line with this, the sociologist Alfred Schutz, the scholar considered to have introduced the phenomenological perspective into social science, argues, for example that "strictly speaking there are no such thing as facts, pure and simple. All facts are from the outset facts selected from a universal context by the activities of our mind [...]. They are therefore always *interpreted* facts ..." (Schutz & Natanson, 1962: 5; our italics).

All variants of phenomenology maintain that subjectivity and interpretation play a crucial role on both the ontological and epistemological levels. This means *inter alia* that realism's sharp distinction between ontology and epistemology becomes somewhat blurred, as there is no access to reality outside of our knowledge or interpretation of it. This is one of the points Schutz makes in the quote above.

The very concept of the "phenomenon"—like many of the other concepts that stem from philosophy and the philosophy of science—has ancient Greek roots. It means "that which appears," but this does not mean that phenomenology assumes that there is a difference between what is real and what is apparent. Subjectivity is accorded such fundamental importance in the phenomenological perspective precisely because the very definition of a phenomenon presupposes that there must necessarily be someone—a subject—for whom the phenomenon comes into view. In other words, there has to be a subject who experiences the phenomenon, otherwise there would be no phenomenon. One of Husserl's groundbreaking principles was that he consciously put parentheses around the question of how things look "in reality" and instead focused on the tangible human experience of the way in which things come into view. What is interesting in this context is that the same object can appear in many different ways.

A key concept in phenomenology is the concept of the *life-world*, which refers to the specific, everyday world that we live in and tend to take for granted. This stands in contrast, for example, to natural science's abstract, systematic and often formalised description of the universe. The life-world is specific in the sense that it is embodied spatially and temporarily. In other words, there is a specific temporal and spatial horizon within which phenomena have a special meaning for those who perceive and experience the world. However, this does *not* mean that we each have our own unique, private experience, and that meaning is a radically individual matter. Rather, the life-world is a *collective* world in which we find ourselves; it is, as Heidegger would put it, the world into which we are thrown. The life-world is a social, cultural and historical context that forms a special horizon of meaning for the individual.

The subject and the subjective experience therefore play a crucial role in a phenomenological perspective. Typically, it is precisely this experience that, in some sense or other, constitutes the object of analysis. This, of course, has consequences for methodology. According to Kvale (1996: 32), phenomenology is about understanding social phenomena from the actors' own perspectives and describing the world as it is experienced by the interviewees. This is based on the assumption that the important reality is the one that people experience. In other words, it is relevant to shed light upon the subjective experience *per se*, and it is less interesting whether it is "true" in an objective sense or what the causes are of this particular experience of a phenomenon. For Kvale, this perspective means, *inter alia*, that an essential element in a method such as the qualitative interview is to "obtain [...] qualitative descriptions of the life-world of the subject with respect to interpretation of their meaning" (Kvale, 1996: 124).

However, it is important to re-emphasise that the interviewee is not seen as an isolated entity, and that the life-world to which he or she refers is collective. Therefore, it is more accurate to say that intersubjectivity is the key aspect in phenomenologically inspired social research.

Meaning is another key concept that is closely related to the concepts of subjectivity and the life-world. As an example with relevance to organisations, the phenomenon of workplace-related stress illustrates the meaning of this concept. The phenomenon can constitute the object of a realist analysis in which stress is viewed as an objective state with very specific characteristics, for example hypertension, insomnia and amnesia. In contrast to this, a phenomenological analysis would effectively be uninterested in what stress actually is—what are "genuine" stress symptoms and who actually, objectively speaking, "has" these symptoms. Instead, a phenomenological analysis would ask how a phenomenon like stress is felt and experienced by employees in their everyday lives—i.e., the way in which stress is part of their life-world. The question of whether, in an absolute sense, the employees are actually stressed or not should effectively be placed in parentheses. In other words, stress is not viewed as an objective phenomenon that exists independently of the subject's experience. Rather, the analysis emphasises the subjective experience of the phenomenon. This means, for example, that stress comprises many different things, as it takes different forms for different people.

While researchers working with a realist perspective are often interested in identifying *causes* and revealing causal relationships, phenomenologists are typically interested in the motives that lie behind actions. Schutz distinguishes between two types of motives: *in-order-to motives* and *because motives* (Schutz & Natanson, 1962: 70). In-order-to motives refer to the future state that the individual seeks to achieve through the action. Conversely, because motives refer backwards in time to past experiences that, according to the individual concerned, cause her to act as she does. For Schutz, it is important that the researcher uncovers the actors' motives in order to understand action and interaction. In this context, a conceptual difference emerges between behaviour and action, and Schutz argues that the social researcher who adopts the phenomenological perspective is interested in the latter. His rationale is:

"What appears to the observer to be objectively the same behavior may for the behaving subject have very different meanings or no meaning at all" (Schutz & Natanson, 1962: 210).

Adopting a phenomenological perspective has a number of methodological consequences. Firstly, the realist ideal of the "neutral researcher" is replaced with an ideal of the researcher who is able to empathise with others' situations and life-worlds. Empathy and insight are often highlighted as essential characteristics of the competent researcher. Despite this shift, the weighting of the ability to empathise can still be

Qualitative Research Methods in Organisation Studies

seen as a form of requirement for researcher neutrality, because phenomenology requires an unprejudiced approach to the area that the researcher makes the object of her study. The point of phenomenology is to examine "the thing itself" without bringing into play any preconceived ideas or explanations. Taking this attitude, past knowledge about the encountered phenomenon should be bracketed "in order to be fully present to it as it is in the concrete situation in which one is encountering it" (Giorgi, 1997: 240). However, the "thing" in question is not the objective, independent research object, but rather the subjective experience and the attribution of meaning in specific life-worlds.

Secondly, phenomenology often focuses on the unique, on specific experiences and perceptions, rather than on general patterns in a larger population. There is a shift from the general to the specific, from the abstract to the concrete. In terms of methodology, this means that there is often an ideal of achieving what the anthropologist Geertz (1973: 5–6) calls "thick descriptions". By extension, Kvale (1996: 145) argues that a good interview is typically characterised by a large number of spontaneous, rich and specific answers. However, at this point there is a certain divergence within phenomenology—Schutz argues, for example, that phenomenological research aims to generalise. However, he is not talking about statistical generalisation, but the typification and formation of ideal types that can be used to understand reality (Schutz & Natanson, 1962: 5f).

Thirdly, phenomenology operates on the basis of a different truth criterion than realism. While realism generally works with a correspondence-theoretical concept of truth, which implies that true knowledge is knowledge that reflects the world as it is *per se,* phenomenology works with a truth concept that might better be described as based on the coherence criterion.

A phenomenological perspective does not stress a particular method, but it is clear that, on the face of it, the perspective is much more suited to a qualitative approach than a quantitative one. This is because the main emphasis is on descriptions of subjective experience, which can be obtained by interviews, focus groups, observation studies and document studies, as we will illustrate in following chapters.

A constructivist perspective

Constructivism is a broad umbrella term covering a variety of different social science perspectives, all of which have in common the fact that they are based on the assumption that our knowledge of the world consists, in some sense or another, of constructions of reality. Constructivism has been disparaged as an exceedingly vague designation, insofar as it brings together a number of very different theories, e.g., symbolic interactionism (Goffman), discourse theory (Laclau & Mouffe and Foucault) and actor-network theory (Latour).

In a constructivist perspective, reality is a construction rather than, as is assumed in realism, an entity that is objective in the sense that it exists independently of the social sphere. An important text in this context is Berger and Luckmann's book *The Social Construction of Reality* (1966), which focuses on how, as humans, we construct our collective reality. Objectified reality is the result of socialy constructed interpretations. Students often encounter the concept of "social constructivism" (e.g., in Berger and Luckmann) rather than just "constructivism." The addition of "social" makes it clear that we are dealing with theories that focus on the construction of reality among humans (who are, of course, social individuals). While all branches of constructivism share the assumption that reality is constructed, the variants do not agree entirely about *who* or *what* constructs it.

According to Collin (2003: 23–24), constructivist literature has three different answers as to who or what constructs reality. First, there are those who, in line with Berger and Luckmann, see everyday social actors as being the ones who drive the construction processes. Second, there are those who focus on how the social scientist herself, via various methods, helps to construct the reality she is attempting to study. This is not entirely contrary to the idea that it is the social actors in everyday life that create reality, but the focus is elsewhere. Third, there are those who downplay the human role as actor and subject in the construction processes, and instead take as their starting point more abstract entities, for example discourses or epistemes (cf. Foucault). For Foucault, therefore, it makes no sense to say that reality is subjectively created, because *both* subjects and objects are created by the discourse.

However, in this context, we will not look any closer at the difference between social constructivism and constructivism, but will focus instead on what it means to work with a perspective that challenges conventional truths and understandings of reality. In general, constructivism claims that what we tend to take for granted—that which seems obvious, natural or necessary—consists of constructions that *could* always have taken other forms. In other words, phenomena are *contingent*; they are historically or socially conditioned (Collin, 2003: 11).

It is important to avoid some of the common misunderstandings of constructivism. Firstly, constructivism does not imply that reality exists only in our minds. In constructivism, too, reality is "out there." It is just not independent of our understanding of it. Secondly, constructivism is not identical to a radical subjectivist relativism, which claims that each of us has our own private truth and perception of the world. On the contrary, constructivists stress that the world is *collectively* constructed. It is precisely collective entities, e.g., language, discourses or objectified institutional structures (Berger & Luckmann, 1966)—that are meaningful and represent the context to which individuals relate.

In general, constructivist analyses have a close focus on language and its role in creating reality. A well-known example of social-constructivist analysis involves the concepts "man" and "woman." In such analyses, the categories "man" and "woman" are assumed to be so laden with cultural meaning—and therefore value—that some researchers choose to use other concepts and neologisms, for example categories such as "managers in men's bodies" and "managers in women's bodies" (Staunæs & Søndergaard, 2008). The point of this type of analysis is that gender often colours other categories, e.g., manager. As Søndergaard (2002: 197) puts it:

> "To talk of subjects with feminine or masculine body signs is, to be sure, a longer and more complicated formulation than simply to say women and men. But it is a deliberate use of an alienating language to constantly remind ourselves that we are here dealing with constructions."

An important objective of constructivism is to show that reality consists of constructions that could always have been different, which means that constructivist analyses have major critical potential. When the status of the knowledge that we take for granted is reversed in constructivist analyses (by the researcher showing how the knowledge we consider to be natural and given was constructed), it is an obvious step to imagine that things actually can (and perhaps even ought to) appear differently. Constructivist analyses are often also called anti-essentialist analyses, precisely because constructivism challenges the essentialism upon which realism in particular is based. Realism assumes that reality has essential, inherent characteristics that exist independently of the person studying them. The opposite is true of constructivism. In his study of the "audit society," which stems from a constructivist perspective, Michael Power (1997) argues, for example, that auditing is a phenomenon that has no essential core or meaning but is shaped into something specific via contingent social and historical processes and practices.

Constructivist analyses adopt an anti-essentialist starting position, which has wide-ranging consequences for methodology. Quantitative methods, which are based on the prerequisite that it must be possible to delineate, stabilise and count the object of analysis, will therefore not be a particularly obvious choice of method for a constructivist analysis. The anti-essentialist approach also means that both interviews and document studies must be seen as methods that reject the idea that an interview can be seen solely as a text with an inherent meaning (the interview's "what"), since the meaning of an interview must also involve the context and the processes surrounding the interview; the design of the project, the research question, role, choice of theory, etc. (the interview's "how") (Järvinen, 2005). Similarly, regarding documentary material, the meaning of the document must incorporate the context; the project design, research questions, role, choice of theory, etc. (Mik-Meyer, 2005).

It is not possible to make a clear distinction between the more social-constructivist variants of constructivism and phenomenology, since both are interested in the intersubjective, in the context and in how meaning is generated. However, since constructivism sees everything in terms of constructions, its object of analysis, by definition, will be fluid, unstable, ambiguous and changeable. For this reason, constructivism does not employ phenomenology's ideal of empathising with the studied individuals' more or less stable life-worlds (Mik-Mey-er & Järvinen, 2005). In addition, constructivism places less emphasis on subjectivity, and focuses to a greater extent on what the different theoretical traditions call, for example, *institutional context* or *discourse*.

One very clear difference between the realist and constructivist perspectives revolves around essentialism. While realism operates with an essentialist approach, an important (perhaps the most important) task for constructivists is to challenge the idea that, fundamentally, everything has one specific and correct classification.

"Every thing has infinitely many points of similarity with every other thing according to which they can be classified; we classify, of course, on the basis of the points of similarity that are of importance to us. In this sense, concepts and classifications are man-made" (Collin, 1998: 51).

The constructivist focus will often be the actual classification process, namely the process that underpins, for example, an organisation associating typically male characteristics with "normal"—perhaps even "good"—executive characteristics. The classification process and the categories to which it leads may be studied and broken down. This facilitates critique of the "natural" categories that we use when we interact with other people, and which we take for granted and seldom call into question (that it is more natural for male managers to be aggressive than it is for female managers).

Perspectives and research questions

Formulating a good research question is crucial to any qualitative study. In other words, the starting point for any study is to define what it is that you want to know. The research question often stems from curiosity. It poses a question about something that you do not understand. Research questions are based on research problems, but it is important to emphasise that, in an academic context, the word "problem" is not quite the same as in everyday language. In everyday life, when we talk about problems, we often mean that there is something wrong. A problem is an undesired condition that can and should be remedied by taking practical action. A practical problem may be that the tyre on your bike is punctured. The solution would be to mend it. A theoretical or research problem differs from a practical, everyday problem. In an academic context, a problem is basically an expression of the fact that you lack knowledge about something in particular—there is something you do not grasp right away, something that sets your mind wondering. As Booth *et al.* (2003: 59) write,

> "a research problem is not motivated by palpable unhappiness, but by incomplete knowledge or flawed understanding. You solve it not by changing the world but by understanding it better."

This means that the formulation of a research question can easily be based on some aspect of the world that, in an everyday sense, is not problematic in the slightest. In this sense, the problem might be understanding why, for example, a particular nursing home has high employee satisfaction and very low levels of staff absence due to illness, in a sector where the opposite would otherwise seem to be the rule. An issue like this might be seen as a problem that forms the basis for formulating a research question because it arouses curiosity and challenges our pre-understanding.

How can we understand the fact that this particular nursing home differs significantly from others when it comes to sick leave? Is it due to the management style, a special "organisational culture" or something else? Conversely, this academic definition of a problem does not, of course, preclude the knowledge generated by the study being used to solve more practical management problems in organisations. Research questions in business schools and university colleges do in fact often take a form that enables others to apply the results in relation to practical problems. The point to bear in mind is that the primary aim of defining a problem is to make it clear that the problem consists of a lack of knowledge or understanding in a given area.

Different theoretical perspectives will lead to different types of research questions. Or, to put it another way, certain types of problems and research questions are better suited than others to the theory that informs the study. "Why" questions ("Why are there not more women in IBM's senior management?") lend themselves to the student seeking to identify and explain causal links, for example, between gender and management. "How" questions ("How do gender and management relate to each other in IBM's senior management?") lead instead toward the processes that affect, for example, gender and management, in order to provide an "understanding" of their interrelationship. "What" questions ("What happens to women when they reach senior management level in IBM?") therefore typically lead to a study that *describes* which factors are important, for example, when the focus is on women and management.

More generally, it might be said that "why" questions lead to analyses that focus on causal relationships in order to provide an explanation, "how" questions lead to analyses that focus on processes with a view to providing understanding, and "what" questions lead to analyses that focus on describing the phenomenon studied. A project's research question typically includes a series of sub-questions to be answered. It is signifi-cant that these sub-questions are logically related to the overall formulation in order to constitute a well-integrated, coherent whole. In this book, we will not go into depth about how best to formulate a research question. Other methodology books contain extended discussion of this question and discuss the difference between the related but not identical concepts of topic, question and research problem (Booth *et al.*, 2003).

We hope that this introductory chapter has clarified why reflection on theoretical perspective is a prerequisite for a suc-cessful project. However, this does not mean that students must choose one of the three perspectives outlined here. There are, of course, other options—and, as mentioned previously, there are also other designations and other ways of drawing the boundaries between the perspectives. The essential point is that assumptions about ontology and epistemology must be thought through carefully, because they have consequences for the study's choice of theory and methodology, as well as implications for the evaluation criteria that it would be rea-sonable to apply when evaluating the quality of the study. In the next chapter, we will therefore discuss which criteria you can use to evaluate what constitutes good methodology in projects that operate with a qualitative approach.

Suggested reading

Reflexive Methodology by Mats Alvesson and Kaj Skjöldberg (2000) presents a number of different perspectives and ways to approach social research in a reflective way. They link ques-tions of methods and methodology with the choice of theo-retical perspective.

The Sage Handbook of Qualitative Research edited by Norman K. Denzin and Yvonna S. Lincoln (2005) gives a thorough introduction to and discussion of qualitative methods. The book contains chapters on different paradigms/perspectives, and methods for data collection and analysis.

Qualitative Research—Theory, method and practice edited by David Silverman (2004) discusses observation (two chapters), texts (three chapters) and interviews (four chapters). Besides providing a concrete introduction to these common qualitative methods, it discusses validity and reflects on qualitative methods applied in an organisational setting, among other themes.

Exercises

1) Discuss why constructivism is often described as anti-essentialism and why, conversely, realism can be described as essentialism.
2) What is the meaning of the concept of "life-world" in phenomenology?
3) Why is it important to relate research questions and theoretical perspective?
4) What is the difference between "what," "why" and "how" questions?
5) Which perspective appeals to you most and why?

CHAPTER 2

Quality criteria and qualitative methodology

Introduction

The discussion about quality criteria and qualitative methodology is a normative one, the key concern of which is how to distinguish between good and less good qualitative studies. What constitutes good qualitative research? How does thinking about methodology help to enhance the quality of the study? While the general consensus is that both research and education would be more or less meaningless without evaluation criteria, there remains some debate about *which* criteria should form the basis for assessing academic work, including student projects. Before you begin to collect data, it is important to consider which quality criteria will apply to the project, i.e., which criteria you would like the readers to use when evaluating whether the project has been well executed. The choice of criteria is closely linked to the theoretical perspective that the study adopts as its starting point.

In this chapter, we discuss some of the most common quality criteria in qualitative social research. We also look at how the different perspectives—realism, phenomenology and constructivism—emphasise and weight different criteria, and how the "same" criteria are often interpreted in different ways within these perspectives. However, what the three perspectives have in common is that they have to relate to objectivity when clarifying which quality criteria have been employed in the study concerned (Peräkylä, 2003: 283).

General quality criteria

Some quality criteria transcend perspectives and, as such, are more generally applicable when evaluating the quality of both research work and student projects. Firstly, there is broad agreement that *coherence* and *consistency* are essential qualities of any well-run project. As a quality criterion, coherence implies an evaluation of the extent to which the component parts of a study are logically coherent. A good study has a clear correlation between, for example, the research questions, the theoretical apparatus and the methodological choices made along the way. The requirement for consistency is related to the coherence criterion. Consistency is also about the coherence of the project but, more precisely, it requires that concepts, methodology and theories be applied in a consequent (consistent) manner throughout the project. In this sense, the consistency requirement is related to a requirement for *precision*. This presupposes *inter alia* that the concepts are clearly defined.

Both coherence and consistency are rooted in the logical requirement of "non-contradiction." In other words, it is problematic to contradict yourself during a study. An example of a methodological contradiction is if a student, on the one hand, operates with a constructivist-inspired premise that there is no objective, unambiguous and independent reality and, on the other hand, uses the interview as a method, assuming that she will gain privileged insights and information that reflect objective conditions that exist independently of the study process.

If the readers of a study are to assess a project's logical coherence and consistency, it is essential that the methodological and theoretical choices made by the researcher or student are both explicit and justified in the text. This requirement results in another quality criterion, often referred to as the *transparency* criterion. The transparency criterion is broad

Qualitative Research Methods in Organisation Studies

and transcends the perspectives, even though it will typically have a different form, for example, in a constructivist-based study than it has in a study based in realism. The criterion implies a requirement that the way in which the student has approached the problem, including why they chose the specific data collection methods used, must be clear to the reader. Why, for example, was the interview method chosen rather than document analysis? Why not choose both? Why were these particular interviewees chosen? How important was the choice of theory for the project's assumptions? What sources of error can be linked to the choice of theory, data and analysis strategy? And so on.

In brief, the transparency criterion means that the final text should state clearly those choices that were made during the project and, in particular, *why* they were made. The outsider looking in on the project has to be able to reconstruct the methodological choices so that it is possible to relate to, and engage critically with, both the project's premises and its findings. And as most of us know from (bitter) experience, it is annoying to have to reconstruct a series of choices when a project is in its final stage, only to learn that it would have been a clear advantage if you had taken these considerations into account at the start and kept them in mind during the project.

Validity and reliability
Most of the traditional textbooks on qualitative methodology highlight the concepts of *validity* and *reliability* as essential quality criteria (e.g., Yin, 2003). Other researchers, particularly in the constructivist tradition, are critical of these criteria and replace them with others such as *relevance* or *polyphony* (meaning that the study should represent as many different voices as possible; for example Hazen, 1993).

Traditionally, the criteria of validity and reliability are defined as follows. Validity is about the extent to which the study's findings actually shed light on the research question, i.e., whether we measure what we say we will measure. Reliability refers to the question of the degree to which the study's methodology is well defined, so that others could, in principle, repeat the study and arrive at the same results. This means that the study may well have a high degree of reliability without this necessarily implying a high degree of validity.

These definitions are very general. In practice, the criteria manifest themselves, and are applied, in a variety of different ways, depending on, among other things, the researcher's theoretical perspective. The criteria are also often specified in a number of sub-concepts. For example, many methodology books operate with different validity aspects and distinguish between construct validity, internal validity and external validity (Yin, 2003: 34)—distinctions we will not dwell upon here.

The validity and reliability criteria are particularly well developed in quantitative research, where they stem from natural science's positivist ideals of strict objectivity. This requires that the study methodology and variables are precisely defined and that the research is influenced as little as possible by contextual factors such as the researcher's role and subjectivity. In this context, reducing *bias* is often at the heart of the matter. Bias refers to any imbalance or colouration of the study's findings due to the actions of the researcher or the actual design of the study.

However, the concept of validity is also often used in qualitative studies, even though the meaning of the concept varies depending on whether it is applied, for example, to realist, phenomenological or constructivist studies. The meaning of the concept of validity is therefore dependent on the research tradition—or perspective—to which the study relates. Often, the concept will be related to the qualitatively based analysis of the data—for example from interviews, documents or observation—upon which the study is based. In this context, validity is about the extent to which the conceptual definition of the phenomena analysed is adequate for what needs to be described (Silverman, 2001: 232ff).

As previously mentioned, the concept of reliability, which in practice often appears to be about the way in which the study's instruments of measurement relate to the data collected, is a quality criterion typically used in positivist or realist studies. These will be studies that, for example, work with hypotheses that can be tested using the correct measuring instruments in order to provide *explanations* (by identifying causal relationships) rather than *understanding*, which is often the purpose of qualitative studies. The reliability criterion implies that it is crucial for a study's findings to be independent of the random events that any qualitative study encounters (Kirk & Miller, 1986). In particular, the criterion is applied in studies that use quantitative methodology, such as surveys or experiments.

In qualitative studies, there has been a debate, sometimes heated, about whether the validity and reliability criteria, which originate from the natural sciences and therefore stem from a more positivist and realist tradition, can be directly applied to projects that use completely different methodologies and are conducted within other perspectives. Some researchers have argued that it is both important and makes good sense to retain the validity criterion, for example, but that it needs to be redefined to be better suited to qualitative research's epistemological focus and methodology. An argument of this type is found, for instance, in Kvale. He argues for a rethinking and reformulation of the concepts of validity and reliability, so that they are meaningful in relation to studies based on, for example, qualitative interviews (Kvale, 1996: 229ff).

Others in the qualitative tradition reject the relevance of the concepts of validity and reliability, and try instead to introduce alternative quality criteria. This means, amongst other things, that constructivist-inspired studies in particular have been criticised for being relativist and undermining the focus on objectivity. This criticism points out quite directly that the more radical constructivist studies consciously reject familiar quality criteria such as validity in their studies. These researchers argue that the research object is *per se* fluid and ambiguous, and can never be detached from its context, including the researcher's or the student's perspective (and theoretical choices). In this light, quality therefore depends on whether or not the researcher includes context-specific factors relevant to the study, namely specific conditions that can be neither quantified nor reproduced by other researchers.

Summary
Regardless of the perspective employed, context plays a different and more prominent role in qualitative studies than in quantitative ones. Where disagreement arises, it is over the question of what and how big a role context will (and ought to) play. As mentioned in the previous chapter, the realist-inspired researcher thinks, in brief, that the actual research context should play the smallest possible role in terms of methodology. Conversely, the constructivist argues that context is always important, and therefore seeks actively to relate to this in her research. Or, to put it another way: in social science analyses, the realist-inspired researcher will strive to draw out descriptions and analyses that can be verified—and, in principle, be reproduced by others—by means of a clearly defined research design, questionnaires, etc., and by opting for veri-

fiable methodology. However, the constructivist-inspired researcher will adapt the research design, interview guide, etc. throughout the process in order to be able to display the requisite sensitivity to the empirical world, and so that the descriptions and analyses are relevant and interesting to users of the study. The phenomenology-inspired researcher places herself halfway between these two points of view.

Although social scientists work with different quality criteria or define the "same" criteria—validity and reliability—in different ways, they generally agree that quality criteria have tangible methodological and practical consequences for a study. For example, the transparency criterion used in many qualitative studies will have consequences for the development of the research question, research design, choice of interviewees, documents, the focus points in participant observations, analysis, strategy and so on.

As the preceding discussion hopefully made clear, each of the perspectives has a different understanding of what constitutes a good project, so we need to look more closely at how "good" research and "well-implemented" methodology are defined in qualitative research.

The remainder of this chapter looks at discussions about evaluation criteria for qualitative studies and relates them to the book's three recurring theoretical perspectives.

Realism and quality criteria

The realist perspective essentially stems from the positivist science tradition and is therefore the perspective that can most easily use typical positivist quality criteria such as reliability and validity, and transfer these to the qualitative research tradition. Validity is about whether the study actually measures what it claims to measure. Reliability is about choosing and specifying measurement methodology and instruments to such an extent that other researchers/students will be able to repeat the study under the same conditions and arrive at the same results. Even though the actual term "research instruments" is derived from quantitative terminology, it is understood here in the broad sense, for example interviews and observations may also be regarded as research instruments.

In a realist perspective, the criterion of generalisability is also often highlighted. Generalisability reflects the desire to generalise a study's findings, which are often rooted in an empirical study of a smaller population (a specific case study), so that the findings also say something about a larger population. If this criterion is applied to a qualitative study (which is typically based on a very small sample that is rarely subjected to statistical requirements for randomised selection), the student must reflect on, for example, how many interviews need to be conducted and who should be selected as representatives of the group being studied. The generalisability criterion is therefore linked to the question of *representativeness*. The assumption is that if a study's results can be generalised to apply to a larger population than the group used as the starting point for the analysis, then those selected for the survey (and their attitudes and views) must be said to be representative of the larger group from which they were selected.

Qualitative researchers are aware that their selected group of interviewees is not representative in a statistical sense (it is not a randomly selected sample) and therefore restricts the opportunities for statistical generalisation. As a consequence, they often work with a concept they instead call *analytical generalisability* (Yin, 2003: 32). According to this concept, generalisation is related to the fact that, in order to ensure consistency, the specific study's results are compared with theory or with other case studies in the same field.

Another quality criterion often referred to in methodology

books is the concept of *triangulation*. This is about adopting more than one angle on the same object of analysis, in order to ensure that the description of the phenomenon at which you have arrived cannot be attributed to a "measurement error." Triangulation is not a quality criterion as such, but a practical way of increasing the study's validity and robustness. Yin (2003: 98f) differentiates between different types of triangulation: data triangulation, investigator triangulation, theory triangulation and methodological triangulation. What we are referring to here is data triangulation. According to Yin, data triangulation is about using different data sources (both interviews and observations) to study the same facts or phenomena. The assumption is that a researcher who uses multiple methods will increase the likelihood that her findings actually reflect the facts in reality and are not a random consequence of, for example, an interview. The study and its conclusions can therefore be said to be more robust. Triangulation is a methodical approach designed to reduce bias.

It is logical that, as a form of quality assurance, triangulation makes particularly good sense in the realist perspective because the realist assumes that the conditions being studied *are*, in a particular sense, "in reality" and that knowledge stems from reproducing the factual circumstances with the least possible distortion. Ontologically speaking, the assumption is that the study's subject matter is stable and exists independently of the study. Triangulation should not be confused with the concept of method combination—this can arise from a desire to triangulate, but it can also fulfil other functions (Mik-Meyer, 2010).

Phenomenology and quality criteria

As mentioned in the previous chapter, phenomenology represents a break with the positivist legacy, and also involves a re-evaluation of classic positivist quality criteria. Phenomenologists are often interested in describing the unique and specific and therefore it is basically meaningless to take as a starting point a criterion such as generalisability, as is the case in realism. In this perspective, what is interesting is not the general pattern but the rich description of specific cases. However, it is possible to reinterpret the requirement for generalisability. For the phenomenology-inspired researcher, then, it is not about the ability to generalise on the basis of findings in a representative sample. Like Yin (2003), Kvale (1996) advocates analytical rather than statistical generalisation, the use of which both authors consider problematic in qualitative studies. However, Kvale's definition of what analytic generalisation involves is less strict than that found in the realist perspective. He refers to the procedure as "a reasoned judgment about the extent to which the findings from one study can be used as a guide to what might occur in another situation" (Kvale, 1996: 233). In line with the phenomenological perspective, Kvale places weight upon interpretation of the potential for the results to be indicative in other instances.

Many phenomenologists argue, however, that, if they are redefined to fit the phenomenological perspective, validity and reliability are also important evaluation criteria in a phenomenologically based study. One variant of validity often highlighted in phenomenology-inspired research is, for example, the idea of *communicative validity*, including *respondent validity*. Kvale (1996: 244) defines communicative validity as "testing the validity claims in a dialogue." In practice, this means that the analysis or parts thereof may be presented to the people who have contributed to the empirical material, for example via interviews. The student gives the interviewees the opportunity to comment on and possibly correct her interpretation of their statements. In other words, the interviewees decide the extent to which they recognise themselves in the analysis, and thereby help to validate its results.

The fact that this criterion is both significant and meaningful in the phenomenological perspective is related to what we referred to in the previous chapter, namely that the phenomenology-inspired study is often designed to obtain descriptions of subjectively based experiences of certain phenomena in a subjective life-world context.

Against this background, the students' ability to empathise becomes an essential attribute. We might even say that validation by the respondent is a form of verification that a sufficient degree of empathy has been employed.

However, the concept of communicative validation extends beyond the respondent. The dialogue about empirical material and the validity of analysis can involve people other than just the interviewees. Typically, dialogue of this kind will involve feedback from other researchers in the field (Kvale, 1996).

The criterion of communicative validation is consistent with the phenomenologist's focus on intersubjectivity, i.e., with the idea that knowledge does not reflect an objective, independent world, but rather relates to the subjects' life-worlds. Against this background, it becomes meaningful to ascertain whether interviewees are able to recognise themselves subjectively in the researcher's description of them in the empirical material. The researcher therefore tests the validity of her material and analysis in relation to subjective rather than objective reality.

Another quality criterion highlighted by many phenomenology-inspired researchers is the more pragmatic criterion, *quality of craftsmanship* (Kvale, 1996: 241). Again, this is a validity criterion that emphasises the intersubjective dimension. This criterion refers to social, intersubjective practice in which a certain consensus has been reached about what constitutes good craftsmanship in research. This criterion is linked to the transparency criterion, in that it must be possible for the reader to gain insight into the choices made during the research process, as well as the reasons why they were made.

Constructivism and quality criteria

Constructivism operates according to a range of different quality criteria that the student can use as the basis for her choice of methodology. Since constructivist research contains a number of very different theories and projects, the quality criteria are also characterised by great diversity. In some projects, the main criterion will be transparency. These projects, like those inspired by realist and phenomenologist perspectives, will explicate and justify the choice of method design, interviewees, approach to analysis and so on. As such, they make visible the underlying premises of the study so that the reader is able to evaluate the choices made. In this sense, we can assert that, for the reader, the project has a high level of credibility if she believes that the choices made were the right ones in relation to the research question.

However, a number of constructivist studies are also informed by quality criteria specific to this perspective, i.e., criteria that are typically not used in realist-inspired research or, to a lesser extent, in phenomenology-inspired projects. What these criteria have in common is that they are highly context-dependent and will be defined locally every time they are used—using, for example, concepts such as *convincing, relevant* or *interesting* (Riessman, 1993). In other words, the argument is that if the study produces relevant and interesting

Qualitative Research Methods in Organisation Studies

knowledge in relation to a defined target group, or if the analyses seem convincing and credible, then the study is of high quality. These quality criteria are, to a high degree, defined by their subjectivity. The personal evaluations of both the reader and the researcher (or student) are therefore relevant in this context.

One criterion often highlighted in constructivist-inspired development is the concept of *reflexivity* (Gergen & Gergen, 2002: 1027). This concept is related to the transparency criterion in the sense that it requires the student to present her reflections openly to the readers. However, the reflexivity criterion goes further, as it requires the student to reflect upon the role that her own position and experiences play in the study.

The premise is that any researcher or student is inevitably situated and positioned in a particular way in relation to her research field, and that this positioning is of crucial importance to the study. In the realist perspective, this would be seen as *bias* or a source of error, but here the positioning is perceived as a condition that the researcher should be aware of and reflect upon. Nor is this condition primarily viewed as regrettable—on the contrary, it is a precondition for particularly interesting analyses as long as the researcher reflects consciously on her own role and position. One—in many people's eyes, somewhat extreme—example of how this translates into real-life qualitative research is found in Ellis and Berger (2002). Here, the research subject's reflections on herself and her relationship to others are the *primary* focus of the article. Other constructivists, however, are critical of this interpretation of reflexivity, and warn that the research risks becoming too "self-indulgent" (Järvinen, 2005: 45).

Some constructivists argue that quality criteria are not separate from ethical criteria. As a result, for example, many qualitative researchers highlight as a quality criterion that many different voices are heard in the study (Gergen & Gergen, 2002). Above all else, there is a focus on making room for voices that are suppressed or marginalised in, for example, official organisational discourse. This is often referred to as a desire for *polyphony* (see Hazen, 1993).

Kvale (1996: 110) introduces a set of "ethical guidelines" to make highly practical recommendations. In this connection, he poses a series of questions to which the student ought to relate when she engages in, for example, an interview-based study. We would like to cite some parts of Kvale's (1996: 112ff) list, which we believe are also applicable to focus-group and participant-observation studies.

Kvale argues that the student must obtain informed consent from the individuals who contribute to the study, and that they must be guaranteed anonymity if they so desire or if the student anticipates negative consequences for the participants if they are not anonymous. He suggests that the student considers who will have access to the material (including during the transcription process) and how the interviewees' anonymity can be ensured during the data-processing stage. He also says that the student must consider how profoundly and critically she will be capable of analysing her data, and whether the study's participants should have the opportunity to read and comment on the analyses before they are published. Finally, he points out that the student must consider how her publishing strategy will affect the study's participants.

Most textbooks on methodology discuss ethics, and emphasise that ethical considerations are an unavoidable and necessary aspect of any study. In this sense, the explication of ethical reflection forms part of the quality evaluation of a study (Eriksson & Kovalainen, 2008: 62ff; Myers, 2009: 45ff).

In this chapter, we have focused on some of the criteria and associated discussions regarding the evaluation of whether a qualitative research project, or a qualitative project conducted by a student, is well done and of high quality. In the next four chapters, we will present four qualitative methods commonly used by researchers and students. These consist of interviews, focus groups, participant observation and document analysis.

Suggested reading
Robert K. Yin's (2003) *Case Study Research: Design and methods* contains reflections on the quality criteria validity and reliability in a realistic perspective. Yin discusses these concepts in relation to the case study, as a particular kind of qualitative study.

InterViews. An introduction to qualitative research interview by Steinar Kvale (1996) discusses quality criteria and links this discussion explicitly to ethics in research projects.

Paivi Eriksson and Anne Kovalainen's (2008) book *Qualitative Methods in Business Research* offers a number of suggestions for how a focus on ethical issues can be used to ensure high quality in research projects and studies.

Exercises
1) Why is it important to reflect on quality criteria when conducting a qualitative study?
2) Define typical criteria for a realist-inspired project and for a constructivist-inspired project. Describe the quality criteria chosen and explain to your fellow students how you can work with them tangibly in a study.
3) Which criteria does phenomenology work with? Explain how and why.

4) Why is it important to be explicit about the quality criteria you have chosen?
5) Discuss which quality criteria you yourself think are the most important in qualitative studies.

CHAPTER 3

Interviews

Introduction

In the vast majority of qualitative research, the student uses one form of interview or another in order to study the given problem. The concept of the interview should be understood in a broad sense, and can be defined as "an inter change of views between two persons conversing about a theme of mutual interest" (Kvale, 1996: 2). Some will consider even this broad definition to be too narrow, because an interview can, of course, involve more than two persons. Multiple interviewers and multiple interviewees can be present during the same interview.

The interview is found in many contexts other than the academic one. Some researchers even talk about us living in an "interview society," in which the interview has become an ever-present way for people to communicate (Gubrium & Holstein, 2002). We are interviewed for jobs, by journalists, at the doctor's and so on. The research interview is related to these other forms but there are some differences, especially in relation to the reflections on methodology to be made in advance of academic work involving interviews. In this chapter, "interview" refers to the research interview.

The interview can take the form of a loosely structured conversation or a rigidly systematic dialogue that follows a carefully designed interview guide (Kvale, 1996). In most cases, an interview will be conducted as a physical meeting at which two people exchange knowledge and experiences. Interviews may also be conducted by email, by phone or in the form of a video conference (Lowndes, 2005; Gillham, 2005). Regardless of the circumstances of the meeting, the interviewer and interviewee will exchange words, and one of them—the interviewer—will have thought in advance about what questions to ask and how the answers will be documented.

In this chapter, we will discuss the preconditions for, and the consequences of, the many choices that the interviewer has to make when she opts to conduct part or all of her data collection by means of the interview method. We will also discuss how the choice of perspective—realist, phenomenological or constructivist—and choice of research question, affects the way in which an interview is conducted. First, however, we shall look more closely at what an interview is and the considerations students must make before choosing for this method of data collection.

Concepts, key questions and theory

An interview can be organised in a more or less structured fashion. There has been considerable discussion about the advantages and disadvantages of unstructured, semi-structured and structured interviews (Eriksson & Kovalainen, 2008: 80).

The *unstructured interview* is defined by the fact that it is primarily the interviewee who is responsible for determining the structure and leading the conversation. In a sense, the term "unstructured" is somewhat misleading, as the interview, inevitably, will have some kind of structure. However, in the unstructured interview, the structure (i.e., the exact nature and order of the questions) is not planned in advance by the interviewer, and the situation gives the interviewee the possibility, to a great extent, to steer the interview's direction and define its content. This approach is often well suited to more exploratory studies, in which the interviewer has little knowledge beforehand of the topic of conversation. It is also a method that can be useful

Qualitative Research Methods in Organisation Studies

when the interview concerns a sensitive issue, in which case a structured interview guide may run the risk of impeding the interviewee's flow and reflections (Gillham, 2005). In the unstructured interview, the interviewer typically poses both "how" and "what" questions (Eriksson & Kovalainen, 2008), but generally lets the conversation flow in whatever direction it takes.

The *semi-structured interview* is defined by the interviewer working from a guide in which the themes and a number of key issues are defined in advance. However, in the interview situation, there is room to deviate from the guide if the interviewee brings up unexpected but interesting topics. According to Gillham (2005: 70), in the semi-structured interview, the interviewer asks all of the interviewees the same open questions (albeit adapted to their particular position in relation to the purpose of the study). The idea is to get all of the interviewees to reflect on the same question, so that the interviewer is able to ensure that an adequate number of supplementary sub-questions are posed in cases where the interviewee provides inadequate responses. There are other interpretations of the semi-structured interview. Kvale (1996) argues that the interview should be adapted to suit the individual interviewee and, as such, his interpretation of the semi-structured interview is less focused on standardisation than Gillham's. Nevertheless, the literature agrees that the semi-structured interview method is suitable for studies in which it is desirable both to adopt an exploratory approach that generates new knowledge and to stimulate interviewees' reflections on a number of pre-selected themes (Fontana & Frey, 2002; Gillham, 2005). Both "how" and "what" questions are also usually posed in the semi-structured interview (Eriksson & Kovalainen, 2008).

The *structured interview* is defined by the interviewer having designed in advance an interview guide that stipulates both the questions and the order in which they will be posed. In this type of interview, therefore, the interviewer is in charge. The structured interview may include open questions, but the interviewer often opts to pose closed questions similar to those also found, for example, in questionnaire surveys. Closed questions are those that are answered by the interviewee selecting an answer from several possible pre-defined response categories presented by the interviewer (Singleton & Straits, 2002). The questions can, for example, be divided into the following three categories: 1) descriptions of the interviewee (which are subsequently used to subdivide the interviewees' responses in relation to age, education, occupation, etc.); 2) behavioural patterns, i.e., what the interviewee prefers (choice of newspaper, political party, etc.); and 3) attitudes, i.e., questions ranked on a scale (0–10) about, for example, an organisation's practices (Gillham, 2005). In the structured interview, the questions are primarily "what" questions (Eriksson & Kovalainen, 2008: 81).

Irrespective of how structured the interview is, it still consists of an exchange of words between two people. The interview differs from a normal conversation in that: 1) the dialogue has an underlying purpose, informed by the research questions on which the study is based; 2) there is a more or less structured interview guide to ensure that relevant data is generated; and 3) roles are determined, such as the interviewer being the person who asks and listens, while the interviewee primarily responds and narrates.

Prior to the interview, it is important to decide how you will document it. In most cases, the interviewer will choose audio recording, but sometimes the topic may be so sensitive that the interviewee does not wish to be recorded. In such cases, the interviewer will have to write the interviewee's answers in a notebook. Most textbooks recommend that you use audio recording, as it is difficult—if not downright impossible—to make sufficiently detailed notes of the conversation for use in the analytical phase. Most also agree that the interview should subsequently be transcribed. How detailed and verbatim the transcript is depends in part on how you wish to analyse the interview material. Since a one-hour interview can take seven to nine hours to transcribe, there may also be pragmatic reasons for choosing to write up only parts of it.

When analysing interview material, it is important to relate to the actual context of the interview, as well as the interaction between the interviewer and interviewee. The context of the interview, including how the interviewer and the interview guide influence the interviewee's narrative, will therefore be a fixed element in the analysis and one to which the student must relate. It could be argued that the interviewer *herself* is just as much of a data collection tool—or a method—as the recording equipment or interview guide. As an interviewer, you will therefore need to reflect upon how your characteristics (gender, age, educational background, etc.) influence the interviewee and what she has to say.

A classic constructivist-inspired text that sees the interview as a situation in which particular empirical material is actively generated is Holstein and Gubrium's (1995) *The Active Interview*. They argue that the interview must not be seen as a passive interviewer–respondent relationship, as both parties jointly and actively create the narrative of the interview. A key point in this context is that the narrative can also be said to be institutional, i.e., the interview is presumed to reflect and reproduce the institutional context. As such, the analysis should never exclusively focus on the content of the actual conversation between interviewer and interviewee.

Irrespective of whether the interview guide is relatively unstructured (themes only), semi-structured (a number of themes and key questions) or highly structured (primarily closed-response categories), most people agree that it is a good idea to gather factual information about the interviewee, for example gender, age, educational background, length of employment, management level, etc. The choices of factual conditions that the interview is designed to reveal must, however, take the study's research question into consideration. Always ask, therefore: What will I use this knowledge for in relation to the purpose of the study? Information about gender, length of employment, and so on, may be relevant and necessary in order to conduct analyses that transcend a series of interviews. For example, it may be interesting to study whether a given attitude to change within an organisation is related to age, gender or position in the organisational hierarchy. It may also be rewarding to look at whether certain attitudes are more prevalent amongst younger interviewees or those with a few years of service in the organisation. However, you should bear in mind that, regardless of perspective, you must be careful when generalising about the background to qualitative material, as it does not comply with the statistical requirement for representativeness in the selection process.

In addition to what we might call personal background information about the interviewee, it is important that the interview guide contains a number of themes that can be developed—more or less systematically—by the interviewee. It is a good idea to formulate these themes as specific questions—and it takes time to think up good questions. Start by brainstorming possible questions. Group them in subject categories, formulate one or two questions in each category (deleting the rest), then pick out questions relevant to the purpose of the study (again), delete some more, and so on. This process may be time-consuming but it is also a prerequisite for a successful interview.

The idea is to produce an interview guide that contains, for example, 10–15 questions that will generate material that the study can use. It is a really good idea to test the guide in advance to ensure that the questions are clearly formulated, easy to understand and do not favour certain types of answers. As a rule of thumb, the shorter the question, the easier it is for the interviewee to respond. Ideally, the interview guide should be tried out on a "real" interviewee, i.e., you should conduct a pilot test in which the interviewee provides answers about the extent to which the questions were easy to understand, relevant or repetitive, whether the order should be changed, and so on. Pilots can be included in the actual study as long as this is taken into account in the student's analysis of the interviewee's comments.

Gillham (2005: 31f) suggests that, before, during and after the interview, the interviewer should be aware of the following points:

Phase 1:	Phase 2:	Phase 3:
Give the interviewee ample opportunity to feel comfortable. Talk about the study's purpose, and explain how you will organise the interview according to themes and how long you expect the interview to last.	Explain in brief the context of your main questions before you pose them. Remember to leave breaks and wait for responses. Be patient and attentive. If the interviewee does not respond after some time, do not suggest answers, but pose questions in a new way. Show interest in the answers. Pose your sub-question(s). Wait before you pose your next main question.	Indicate that the interview is coming to an end. Show that you are satisfied with the result. Check against your interview guide to ensure that you have received answers to all of your questions. Ask the interviewee if she has anything that she wishes to add. Thank the interviewee for her time and tell her when she will hear from you again.

There are a number of choices associated with conducting interviews. You must decide which form of interview—unstructured, semi-structured or structured—is liable to produce responses that shed light on the problem being studied. You have to develop, and preferably test and adapt, your questions. You have to decide whether the actual interview will take the form of a personal meeting or whether it will be conducted by phone or email. You have to decide how many people to interview, and identify the relevant people. You have to choose recording equipment and decide on a method of transcription.

Once the interview material has been transcribed, a number of further choices are associated with their subsequent analysis. If you opt for a systematic, theme-based reading of the interview, then you will have to choose which theoretical concepts will help to establish the themes you want to discuss. If you choose a more inductive approach, you will need to establish coding categories. These can be determined after reading one or two interviews, and then applied to all of the material. You can also choose a more interpretive reading, which is neither systematically based on organisational themes nor based on inductively embedded categories, but is instead determined, for example, by the problem. In other words, a number of choices are associated with the subsequent processing of the interview material (see Myers, 2009: 165ff for a list of methods of analysis).

Finally, the interviewer is faced with certain ethical considerations. In line with the discussions about quality criteria in Chapter Two, many textbooks recommend that you are open about the purpose of the study when talking to potential interviewees. For example, it is suggested that you tell them how you will store, analyse and use the recorded interview (Gillham, 2005: 10). The aim is that the interviewee should be told—preferably in writing—who will be allowed to listen to/ read the interview, how anonymity will be guaranteed, how it will be ensured that the interview is stored safely, which publications it is envisaged will publish the interviews, how the student will handle any media interest, and so on (Gillham, 2005: 13).

Perspectives—implications

Frequently, the distinction between the "what" and the "how" of the interview is used to highlight the fact that an interview can be read with the focus on either what it says something about (content of meaning) or how it says it (production of meaning) (Holstein & Gubrium, 2004: 142). To put it another way, it is about the assumed weighting of the importance of the context—the purpose of the study, the interview guide, etc.—in relation to the interviewees' attitudes and experiences, and whether the effect of the context is viewed as a potential source of error (bias) or as an interesting aspect of the analysis. Realist-inspired studies will be more interested in the interview's "what" and see the context as "noise" that ought to be reduced as much as possible in order to ensure a high degree of validity and reliability. Constructivist-inspired analyses, on the other hand, will often have an interest in analysing the interview's "how." The latter type of analysis, therefore, has a stronger focus on context than the former.

Kvale uses the metaphors *miner* and *traveller* to illustrate two very different perceptions of the role and purpose of the interviewer. If the interviewer is seen metaphorically as a miner, this brings to mind a process in which the interview is about digging out valuable knowledge or meaning ("precious metals") from your interviewees ("the mine that contains the buried metal"). This image is particularly associated with the perspective that we have chosen to call the realist perspective. In this sense, the interviewee appears as a subject with embedded knowledge, and would ideally remain unaffected by the miner's (the interviewer's) digging/questioning technique.

The traveller, on the other hand, suggests someone who is curious, whose conversation with the interviewee creates a joint narrative in a universe of interpretation (Kvale, 1996). This metaphor is better suited to the two perspectives described in this book as phenomenology and constructivism. These metaphors illustrate how an interviewer can operate with very different assumptions about the nature of knowledge. The miner perceives knowledge as something that already exists in a strictly delineated form "out there," it exists independently of the interviewer and her study. This is the same image that is implied when you talk about "collecting data." By comparison, the traveller perceives knowledge as something that is formed only during the actual conversation.

Even though it is difficult to unambiguously delineate the book's three perspectives—realism, phenomenology and constructivism—we will nevertheless try to outline some of the implications of the choice of perspective for the interview-based study.

Realism

In realist-inspired studies, the ideal is objectivity, dispassionate knowledge that can be verified and controlled and is ideally unaffected by personal attitudes and prejudices. Kvale's metaphor of the miner reflects this perception. This ideal has direct consequences for both the planning and conducting of an interview study. In relation to realism's quality criterion of producing reliable and generalisable results, all things being equal, a structured interview guide will increase both the reliability and the generalisability of the outcome of the study.

Qualitative Research Methods in Organisation Studies

In the realist perspective, a structured interview guide with delineated, closed response categories is perceived as minimising the interviewer's influence on the interviewee—this is often referred to as *the interviewer effect*. It might also be said that the influence of intersubjectivity, which can be seen as the basis for an interview situation, is minimised as far as possible by using a structured guide that attempts to reduce the interviewer's influence on the interviewee.

The ideal of objectivity also means that, even in more exploratory studies with open questions, the questions must be posed in the same way to all interviewees in order to ensure that they have the same impact and that, as far as possible, the study is independent of local contextual conditions. It is also appropriate for the same person to conduct all of the interviews, and for the rest of the physical parameters to be as uniform as possible.

In the realist-inspired study, there is also an assumption that the interviewee possesses knowledge about the issue upon which the study is focused (cf. the interview's "what"). In the analytical phase, the "what" of the interview will therefore automatically enjoy precedence over the "how"—not because it is assumed that the processes surrounding the interview situation have no influence on the conversation, but because the study has been organised in a way that seeks to minimise the influence of these conditions upon the interview as far as possible.

Phenomenology

In phenomenology-inspired studies, the aim is that the students understand rather than explain social phenomena; that they understand them from the actors' own perspectives and describe them in the way the actors experience them. The point is to describe reality as people perceive it. This ideal places the actor's life-world right at the heart of the analysis, which has consequences for the actual interview. The interviewer's role is to ensure that the interviewee is afforded the opportunity to describe the reality that surrounds her in as accurate and detailed a manner as possible, without slipping into explanations and analyses.

The interviewer will therefore typically pose open questions aimed at extracting examples from the interviewee's everyday life. The aim is to obtain descriptions that are sufficiently detailed so as to enable analysis of the interviewee's life-world and the way in which she sees her reality. Phenomenology's focus is on obtaining direct subjective descriptions because, as mentioned previously, the idea is to try to understand a given context. While the interviewer inspired by the realist perspective typically follows a structured guide, it makes more sense for the student inspired by phenomenology to use a semi-structured guide.

The phenomenological perspective does not, therefore, operate with an ideal of objectivity that is understood as the uncovering of verifiable knowledge that exists "out there" (see above); nor is it the interviewer's role to judge whether a given experience is "real" or not. The interviewer does not, for example, ask questions about the extent to which the interviewee is "right" or "wrong" when she states that she considers her company's management style to be dictatorial. The interviewer's role is to help the interviewee—by means of an empathetic interview technique—to talk about her everyday life and experiences without feeling inhibited or steered in a particular direction. An important goal of the interview situation is therefore to establish an open-minded space in which the interviewee is able to express herself confidently and freely. However, in relation to methodology, it is also important to note that the life-world concept is not personal, but collective.

Qualitative Research Methods in Organisation Studies

Thus, the knowledge that you derive from an interview does not just reflect an individual's personal experiences, but can also be seen as an example of collective workplace experience as reported by the interviewee.

The concept of intersubjectivity is central to the phenomenological perspective precisely because it assumes that knowledge is created and developed between people, and as such it can be linked both to the shared world to which the interviewee belongs, and to the interviewee's personal experience. In terms of interview technique, the interviewer must therefore also reflect on the way in which she influences the interviewee. In contrast to the realist perspective, mutual influencing is seen as an inevitable condition of human interaction, including in interview situations.

Constructivism

In constructivist-inspired studies, the ambition is to produce knowledge that illustrates the complexity, ambiguity and instability that characterise the social world. The assumption, which is an extension of the phenomenological perspective, is that knowledge is dependent upon perspective and is (continuously) constructed in social processes. Since knowledge is not assumed to be embedded in the individual like a substance or essence just waiting to be extracted (during an interview), the context (focus on the production of meaning) assumes a central role (Holstein & Gubrium, 1995). The constructivist study, therefore, pays greater attention to how the project design, interview guide, questioning techniques, physical location of the interview, and so on, affect the interview itself, and thus the interviewee's narrative (Järvinen, 2001), than is the case in the phenomenological perspective (which pays less attention) and the realist perspective (which pays the least attention). There is also a greater awareness than in the other two perspectives of how dominant social narratives (discourses/institutional factors) influence the actors.

In constructivism, it is assumed that the individual is a social actor who will adapt her actions to (any new) social reality—including the interview situation. Within this perspective, little faith is placed, for example, in structured interviews with response categories developed by the interviewer. This is precisely because the aim is to gain insight into the ambiguity and instability that is assumed to characterise all social phenomena. In the constructivist perspective, structured interviews, therefore, only help to reproduce the study's assumptions about the social reality being studied, and do not help generate new knowledge (Järvinen, 2001).

Precisely because constructivist-inspired studies focus so much on the impact of context on empirical material, it is also the perspective in which there is a great deal of discussion about how the interview is affected by the interviewer's behavior, gender, age, educational background, and so on.

As was established in Chapters one and two, it is sometimes difficult to draw a clear line between the phenomenological perspective and the constructivist perspective, because both focus on intersubjectivity and how knowledge is created between people (relation) and not in people (essence), cf. the term "active interviewing" (Holstein & Gubrium, 1995; 2004). However, in terms of methodology, the two perspectives differ when it comes to the role of the interviewer. While the interviewer inspired by phenomenology will seek to infuse the situation with empathy and insight in order to gain access to the interviewee's life-world, the interviewer inspired by constructivism will choose a different strategy because she assumes that it is not possible to gain access to another person's life-world and map out her motives (Schultz, 1962). The constructivist-inspired interviewer will also ask open questions, but she will not think that empathy, in the form of empathic listening and questioning, will provide insight into the motives for the interviewee's actions, etc., which is an important objective of analyses inspired by phenomenology.

Case study: Human resource management (HRM)

In the case that we have chosen as an example of the interview method, Mik-Meyer (2009) used not only the research interview but also limited participant observations and document analysis. Part of the material also consisted of recorded conversations about health issues between overweight individuals and health consultants (Mik-Meyer & Villadsen, 2012). These conversations could be considered interview material, even though the interviews were conducted by health consultants. However, as they are not research interviews, the health discussions will be considered a kind of observation material.

The two interview excerpts cited as examples are taken from interviews with executives from ten different public and private sector companies, in which the companies' health initiatives are discussed.

The study itself basically adopted a constructivist perspective on health and weight. The ambition was to see how the issues of health and weight were discussed among managers and overweight employees. The interviews with the managers in the case study focused on how overweight employees were identified as a problem group whom the company saw it as their duty to help. The study therefore had no realist-inspired interest in finding out if the companies' actions in this area helped employees lose weight or not.

Although the study could thus be said to be exploratory, since Mik-Meyer wanted to explore attitudes to weight problems, the interview guide was semi-structured and piloted in advance. The interview guide was built up around ten key questions, including questions about the interviewees' age, number of years in the position they occupied at the time of the interview, and their educational background. The purpose of this information was to provide a context for the responses and data analysis. The interviews were transcribed in full, and individual interviewees were allowed to inspect and approve them. The audio files were anonymously stored on Mik-Meyer's computer, and physically locked in an office cupboard. Here is an excerpt from an interview with a manager of a large Danish company.

INTERVIEWER: Do you think the great media focus on the problem makes it easier for overweight employees to talk about their weight [...] the fact that you can be both healthy *and* overweight?

MANAGER: Of course you can be healthy and overweight. You can also be thin and unhealthy. We can't do any more than just say that there's this course, oh and by the way the canteen food is healthy. Or, you could always exercise. We can try to do something about stress. We can try, structurally, to provide frameworks that are healthy. But we can't really do much more than that.

INTERVIEWER: That was actually my last question ...

MANAGER: The weight issue is a difficult one. People say you shouldn't stigmatise and medicalise people, so that's obviously something we talk about, that we take into account.

INTERVIEWER: Medicalise and stigmatise, you say—have you ever witnessed employees being medicalised?

MANAGER: No, I don't think you'll get anybody to say that—not anybody who works with health promotion anyway—but it happens, though, even if it isn't the idea.

This excerpt begins with a main question about the impact of the increased media focus on weight on people who are overweight, and about the link between being overweight and healthy. In terms of interview technique, it is not ideal that two questions are asked at the same time. More general questions that require analysis by the interviewee, as opposed to mere description, can also be difficult to answer.

As the response shows, the manager balks at analysing the issue (of media and weight) but chooses instead to respond based on workplace experience, and gives a broad but also specific response (cf. her use of "we" and "you"). Ideally, the interviewer should pose the main question again since it has not been answered, but chooses instead to begin the third stage of the interview and launches into a closing comment. The manager responds by bringing up two themes that have been discussed earlier in the interview (and around which a number of questions have revolved). The interviewer then gathers together the two central concepts of "medicalisation" and "stigmatisation," hoping to get the manager to reflect further on these two key concepts.

The excerpt illustrates the exploratory approach to discussions of health and weight that formed the starting point for the study. This exploratory approach makes open, process-oriented questions the obvious choice. Open questions that are largely related to the interviewee's responses (as illustrated in the interviewer's questions about medicalisation and stigmatisation) are obvious choices in constructivist- and phenomenology-inspired studies designed to generate understandings of a phenomenon, with a focus on how the phenomenon is spoken about in a range of contexts. If the study had been based on realism, and if it had focused on providing an explanation of why companies work with health initiatives for employees with weight issues, an exploratory approach with a very open interview technique would not have been such an obvious choice. In such cases, the interviewer would use a more structured interview guide. This would ensure the acquisition of certain knowledge in order to provide a (causal) explanation of the "why" question.

Let us turn to a second excerpt from the same study, from an interview with a manager of another large, private Danish company.

INTERVIEWER: Weight issues and obesity are not new concepts as such. Is it perhaps new that we talk about them so much? Do you think there's been a shift?

MANAGER: Yes, I think there has been a shift, but it's a general one. I mean, I don't think so much in relation to obesity and being overweight. We're very much moving into—the whole organisation—focusing on ensuring that the individual has responsibility in the broadest sense, responsibility both for his work and himself. There's a convergence of interests, so of course the company wants to support individuals taking responsibility for themselves and their lives, including their weight. So I think that, in terms of attitudes, we are engaged in a process. A decade ago, the thinking was very much that if I had a problem, then it was the company's problem. Nowadays, there is probably a little more subtle attitude, along the lines of: "I'm well aware that I have a major stake in this—call it my career or my weight problem." People have a far better understanding that it's not only the company's responsibility, but also the employee's. [...]

INTERVIEWER: Do you think it's hard for overweight people? I mean, it's a very personal thing. They may have low self-esteem ...

MANAGER: There's no doubt that a lot of overweight people suffer from low self-esteem. They probably lack the resources to take responsibility for their own situation, otherwise they'd have done so ages ago. They've probably done everything they could. I don't think anybody wants to be overweight. So I suppose we might do something anyway—to get to grips with the problem, if I can put it like that. Because they probably won't manage it on their own. Most people at the top looking down would say that.

The interviewer's first question illustrates the presentation of a (normative) context that forms the framework for the actual main question ("Do you think there's been a shift?"). Note that the manager chooses to answer the question that was posed last, which often happens in interviews when you ask more than one question at a time. This highlights the appropriateness of always asking just one question at a time. We have chosen to include the whole of the manager's response, as he does something interesting.

He introduces into the interview a third party, who speaks as if he himself is one of the overweight employees (cf. "I'm well aware ..."). You might therefore argue that there are not two voices present in this interview, but three: the interviewer, the manager and a representative of the group of overweight employees. A constructivist analysis would incorporate and adopt an analytical approach to all three voices (to ensure complexity and ambiguity) because the third voice shows, in a very direct manner, the way in which the manager assumes overweight people look at themselves and their responsibilities. As mentioned, the study aims to provide an understanding of how the relationship between health and weight problems is constructed in a particular context (the workplace). As such, all statements capable of promoting such an understanding of this phenomenon are, in principle, interesting to the constructivist.

The criterion for whether a given statement is interesting in this context is whether the statement adds knowledge to the understanding of the relationship between health and weight. As such, whether or not the statements represent reality—i.e., whether the manager's description of overweight people and how individuals in this group see themselves is true (in a correspondence-theory sense) or not—will never be a criterion. It is therefore irrelevant whether the manager is correct in his description of overweight employees' views of themselves. If, however, the study had been realist-based and had been intended to provide an explanation, then the selection criteria used to determine which statements would be used in the analysis would have been different. In such a situation, statements that are capable of stimulating an explanation of the phenomenon would be used. Based on this criterion, a manager's interpretation of how overweight people see themselves would be irrelevant. Let us return to the interview.

The interviewer follows up with a question about whether the manager believes that overweight people have a self-esteem problem. This follow-up question (rather than a main question from the semi-structured interview guide) is a leading one, and introduces the concept of self-esteem. As Järvinen (2005) has pointed out, in their desire to focus on the interview's "how" (the interaction between interviewee and interviewer), many constructivist-inspired studies almost forget the "what" (what the interviewee has to say about the issue being studied). If you take this criticism at face value, and choose to focus on what the interviewee actually says, you will be able to problematise the fact that it is the interviewer who introduces the concept of "self-esteem."

In her exploration of the interviewee's life-world, which is the ambition underlying a project inspired by phenomenology, the interviewer could usefully have formulated the question as one of responsibility ("Is it lack of responsibility among the overweight that means they are unable to lose weight?"), since this is the concept that the manager himself cites. Phenomenologically speaking, it would be most fruitful for the analysis to use the interviewee's own descriptions. This would underpin an empathy with the interviewee's life-world, and also stimulate his ability to maintain and vary his experiences of the phenomenon he is describing. In a phenomenological perspective, the example of interview technique given above is therefore problematic, as the interviewee's answers perhaps reveal more about the interviewer's life-world (i.e., the assumption of a relationship between being overweight and having low self-esteem) than the interviewee's.

From a realist perspective, the ideal interview situation would be one in which the interviewer's own attitudes and experiences influence the interviewee as little as possible. Leading questions—as illustrated in this extract—are therefore also problematic in this perspective.

In a constructivist perspective, the leading question is not a problem *per se*, since the criterion here is rather whether the technique leads to answers that shed interesting light on the problem. The exchange between interviewer and interviewee on the concept of "self-esteem" thus illustrates Holstein and Gubrium's (1995, 2004) point, that the interview is an active process of generating meaning, in which both parties—interviewer and interviewee—jointly create a narrative that also reflects an institutional idea of what it means to be overweight. In this context, leading questions are not necessarily a problem.

Summary
In this chapter, we have attempted to outline a number of factors of which students should be aware and upon which they should reflect, when and if they choose to use qualitative in-

terviews as a method. The case study used to illustrate the interview method stems from a constructivist-inspired research project, as illustrated by the very open, process-oriented questions posed by the interviewer. Although we have only cited very short interview excerpts from a large volume of qualitative material, the questions indicate the fact that what is being sought is not unambiguous, fixed knowledge about a given phenomenon, but rather reflections on a topic such as being overweight or the relationship between being overweight and a number of other conditions (media interest, low self-esteem, etc.). The excerpts are also selected to illustrate how aspects of this approach can also be viewed as a source of error in a realist perspective, or as an example of a less successful interview in a phenomenological perspective.

Just because we say the questions are typically constructivist- or phenomenological-inspired does not mean, of course, that a realist-inspired project will not also be capable of seeking out similar reflections and thoughts. However, the realist's interview technique would aim to uncover and elicit definitive answers that reflect an objective reality in a valid manner. The interviewer would probably also spend more time on each question in order to get more complete and unambiguous answers.

In this chapter, we have also pointed out that it is time-consuming to devise and conduct a well-planned interview-based study. Some researchers argue that, on average, you should expect it to take over 20 hours to plan, conduct, transcribe and code an interview that lasts one hour. If you conduct a small study with only a few interviews, which would be the norm for student projects, the number of hours spent increases in line with the preparation factor per interview (Gillham, 2005: 27).

In other words, it is time-consuming to conduct a well-planned interview-based study in which the perspective is linked to the research question, which in turn is related to the choice of interviewees, the degree of structuring in the interview guide and the choice of questions. Conversely, however, you will discover that it is much more time-consuming—and frustrating—to engage in an interview-based study if you have not prepared it carefully and reflected on what you want to achieve.

Suggested reading

Steinar Kvale (1996) *InterViews. An introduction to qualitative research interviewing* is a good basic textbook introduction to interviews based primarily on a phenomenology perspective. It provides both a theoretical foundation for understanding interviews and a series of practical instructions for conducting them.

Bill Gillham's (2005) *Research Interviewing: The range of techniques* discusses many different types of interviews—including telephone interviews, email interviews and video interviews—in a highly practical and understandable way.

James Holstein and Jaber Gubrium's (1995) book *The Active Interview* is a classic text with a particular focus on the intersubjective and institutional aspects of the interview situation. Much recent interview research refers to this text, which represents a serious break with the perception of the interview situation as a technique that "collects data" and is therefore critical of both the realist and the phenomenological approach to the interview.

Exercises

1) Formulate three different research questions—related to a realist, a phenomenological and a constructivist perspective—for a project that will examine companies' health initiatives for overweight employees, and discuss whether the interview would be a suitable method for elucidating these issues.

2) Based on the case study in this chapter, formulate three-to-four realist-inspired interview questions for a manager responsible for her company's health initiatives.

3) Identify typical sources of error in the realism-, phenomenology- and constructivism-inspired interview study. Does it make sense to speak of "sources of error" in all three perspectives? Why or why not?

4) What ethical considerations should be included in an interview study?

5) What is a leading question? Is it problematic to ask leading questions in an interview? Justify your answer.

CHAPTER 4

Focus groups

Introduction

Focus groups are a special kind of group interview used with increasing frequency by qualitative researchers in a wide range of fields, especially since the 1980s. Particularly popular in marketing, communications and media research, focus groups have also gradually gained ground in new research fields as diverse as human resource management (HRM), financial management and strategy. However, as a method, focus groups are still significantly less prevalent than individual interviews—which, as mentioned in the previous chapter, are used in the vast majority of qualitative studies. Apart from marketing and communications research, focus groups are not much used in organisational studies.

Focus groups involve the researcher or student bringing together a number of people who are then interviewed as a group or invited to discuss a range of themes. Focus groups are therefore designed to procure qualitative empirical material from a group interview that is controlled by a researcher or a student, and structured around one or more themes defined in advance by the researcher/student. The method includes aspects of both observation studies and the qualitative interview. The focus group is similar to the qualitative interview in that participants are asked to respond to a series of questions or topics posed by the researcher or student.

Most researchers agree, however, that the purpose of the focus group, as opposed to the individual interview, is not to delve into individual responses in depth (Eriksson & Kovalainen, 2008: 172). Instead, what is significant is the dialogue and interaction within the group, particularly the participants' responses to what their fellow participants say. This is where the focus group is reminiscent of the observation study, because both methods focus on social interaction. Accordingly, many researchers stress that a focus group should not be thought of as a group *interview*, but as a group *discussion* (Halkier, 2002). However, there is no consensus on this in the methodology literature. To some extent, it depends on whether you are working from a constructivist, phenomenological or realist perspective.

While the literature—regardless of theoretical perspective—agrees that there is a difference between group interviews in general and the *focus* group interview specifically, there is far less consensus when it comes to what, exactly, counts as a focus group. Some advocates of the focus-group method claim that a number of criteria (for group composition, conduct, etc.) must be met before a group interview can be classified as a real focus group. Others operate with a more inclusive definition that is less focused on defining narrow limits for what counts as a focus group and what kind of group interview falls outside this category (Morgan, 1996).

While it is impossible to date accurately the emergence of the focus group as a separate method, there is a degree of consensus that American sociologists Merton and Kendall's 1946 article "The Focused Interview" was groundbreaking in terms of introducing the method to the social sciences. It also indirectly lent its name to the method. Focus groups have, for some time, been hugely popular outside academia, and are used for commercial purposes by pollsters, advertising companies and consultants. It is therefore easy to find manuals and guidelines that set rules of thumb for working with focus groups and offer tips and tricks about everything from group composition to physical setting. However, it is important to distinguish between the focus-group industry and the research context. The latter has its own distinct purpose and a different kind of thinking about methodology. Theoretical considerations ought to play a more prominent role in academic work.

This chapter will not set out specific guidelines for working with focus groups, therefore, but will instead discuss a range of practical, methodological and theoretical issues that arise in connection with this particular method. As we have done in the previous chapters, we will also discuss the implications of the choice of theoretical perspective, because focus groups also differ depending on whether you work with them in a realist, phenomenological or constructivist framework.

Concepts, key questions and theory

As mentioned above, focus groups constitute a method that might be described as halfway between interview and observation. The method is similar to other types of interview in the sense that the researcher or student brings together a number of individuals in order to elicit their responses to a series of questions. These responses then provide the qualitative material that forms the basis for subsequent analysis. When focus groups are based on a constructivist or phenomenological perspective, the similarities with the methodology deployed in observation studies are noticeable because observation and analysis of internal interaction and discussion in the group will be a key component. In this sense, the purpose of the focus group is not only to analyse *what* the group members say, but—just as importantly—*how* they relate to each other and, not least, to what the other participants say.

Group dynamics in the interview situation mean that the discussion in the focus group, and therefore the empirical material it generates, amounts to more than the sum of a series of simple statements (Morgan, 1996: 139). One of the special features of the focus group is that its participants account for, argue for and perhaps even defend their points of view in dialogue with the other participants, and they will typically also ask questions to each other. In this way, the participants are encouraged to explicate assumptions and norms that would remain "tacit" in many other contexts (Bloor *et al.*, 2001). In extension of this, there may be a particular analytical interest in observing how agreement is established and disagreement is handled within the group. The focus group often provides opportunities to gain insight into how certain norms come to be accepted by the group and thus control the discussion of a particular issue (Halkier, 2002).

One academic who has dealt extensively with focus group methodology in a social research context is David Morgan, who defines the focus-group interview as "a research technique that collects data through group interaction on a topic determined by the researcher" (Morgan, 1996: 130). This short definition points to several of the characteristic aspects of focus groups and distinguishes the method from other qualitative approaches. Firstly, the interview (to the extent that there actually is one) involves a *group* of people, who together relate to the topics the interviewer brings up and the questions she poses. The focus group differs from other groups in several ways. The focus group is often only a group *because* it is brought together as one by the researcher. Against this background, Merton (1987) asserts that it is actually misleading to speak of it as a group. In other words, the group is set up specifically for use in a particular research project and is therefore rarely a "natural" group in the sociological meaning of the concept, but rather a "temporary group" (Merton, 1987: 555). However, it is not an invariable rule that the participants must not know each other in advance. On the contrary, in certain contexts it may be an advantage if the participants know each other in advance, and perhaps even constitute an established group in the sense that Merton attributes to the concept. Some of the more prescriptive focus-group manuals have a tendency to specify both the composition and the number of participants in a group, but there is no consensus in the literature about the ideal number of people in a focus group. As with all other questions of methodology, this is very much dependent on what the student wishes to achieve, which in turn is closely related to the problem the study addresses and the perspective that it has adopted.

Secondly, the very concept of *focus* is a defining characteristic of the focus-group method. Morgan stresses that the interaction in the group is based on one or more issues determined in advance by the researcher, whose function also includes ensuring that the conversation remains focused. For this reason, the role of the interviewer in a focus group is often referred to as the *chair, moderator* or *facilitator.* This designation also underlines the fact that the key focal point is the internal interaction between the participants, rather than the interaction between the participants and the interviewer. However, in order not to confuse concepts, this chapter will refer consistently to the researcher/student as the interviewer.

As previously mentioned, *interaction* is a key concept in relation to focus groups. The observations of interaction in this context, however, are different from typical ethnographic observations, which are made in "natural" settings. In the focus group, the observed interaction takes place in an artificial framework established by the researcher. In that sense, the method more closely resembles a form of social experiment (Demant, 2006: 131).

When working with focus groups, the student has to consider a whole series of practical questions in advance. How many people will be in the group? What will be the composition of the group? Where will they meet? What is the best way to prepare for the interview, and how active a role will the interviewer play in conducting and chairing the meeting? How many different focus groups will there be in the study concerned? Will focus groups be combined with other methods (e.g., individual interviews, observations or document studies)? How will the discussions be recorded in such a way that empirical material is procured and is in a useful format? How will this empirical material be analysed?

As mentioned previously, specific answers to these questions are closely related to the research question and theoretical perspective. However, before we start to discuss the implications of the various perspectives, we will briefly stress and discuss some of the general, practical questions that must be addressed by the student who wishes to work with focus groups.

The number of participants in a group can vary considerably. It partly depends, as mentioned, on the purpose of the focus group. According to the literature, the number of participants can vary from 3–4 to 10–12. If the group is any larger than that, it runs the risk of dividing into subgroups, in which case it can become difficult to maintain focus. Large groups also make the subsequent analysis work more difficult, because the material will have a tendency to be extremely complex and difficult to put into some kind of order (Halkier, 2002: 38). On the face of it, it might be said that if the purpose of the focus group is to elicit many different points of view, it may be an advantage to have a relatively large number of participants. Conversely, a small group would be able to consider individual issues in greater depth, and interaction in a small group is also more easily analysed afterward. According to Halkier (2002: 39), large groups are primarily suitable for analyses that weight the participants' opinions, while smaller groups are better suited to analyses that emphasise interaction within the group. Several writers point out that in cases where the issue under discussion is a sensitive one, a large group can be a disadvantage, as it may inhibit some participants.

Another significant question concerns the composition of the focus group. *Who* should take part in the group? The focus-group interview is a qualitative method. As such, the respondents are not chosen according to the selection principles used in quantitative methods, which are designed to guarantee representativeness and generate statistics that can be extrapolated to a larger population. In other words, the focus group is *not* a random sample. However, precisely because the group dynamics are often the interesting aspect from an analytical point of view, it is crucial to reflect upon which criteria will determine the composition of the group. Should the group be relatively homogeneous, so that, for example, participants in a market-research survey are from the same segment of the market, or should it include people from different segments? Another important question, as previously mentioned, is whether the participants should know each other in advance, or whether the meeting in the focus group should be their first encounter.

The obvious answer to both questions is, yet again, that it depends upon the research question and perspective. It is sometimes crucial to select participants that form a relatively homogeneous group, while in other cases the point is that the group is heterogeneous. If homogeneity is important, then you must, of course, define more precisely which aspects you want to be uniform. Do you want participants of the same gender, age or ethnic background? Is there an existing theoretical definition, based on a combination of characteristics, which places a participant in a particular market segment? In relation to positions within an organisational hierarchy, is it a requirement that everybody who takes part in the focus group is, for example, a middle manager?

The same applies to the question of whether the participants should know each other in advance. For example, in her study of attitudes toward food and associated health risks among families with small children, Halkier (2002) decided to let people who knew each other in advance be part of the same focus group, because she was interested in studying intersubjective dynamics. Her assumption was that these would also play an important role in the participants' daily lives. Somewhat bluntly put, it might be said that studies based on a realist perspective would tend toward people not knowing each other in advance, because when people already know each other there is a particularly strong risk of them influencing each other in an unsuitable manner and not responding "honestly." Conversely, researchers rooted in phenomenology and constructivism often see it as an advantage for the participants to know each other in advance (Demant, 2006), precisely because they are more interested in how people affect each other in group processes.

The question of where to hold the actual group meeting is sometimes considered important. Pollsters and others in the commercial sphere who work with focus groups often go to considerable lengths to design special rooms (with specially mounted video equipment and one-way mirrors) to make it possible for people other than the interviewer (typically, the person who commissioned the study) to observe the actual interview. In principle, and regardless of perspective, researchers agree that the location is significant and constitutes a specific framework for the meeting (e.g., Bloor *et al.*, 2001: 38). However, this discussion will in most cases be less relevant

Qualitative Research Methods in Organisation Studies

for the student, who typically needs to take a more pragmatic view and often conducts the focus-group interview where it is possible, for example in rooms made available by the organisation being studied or at her own educational establishment.

More relevant and practical questions for both researcher and student are related to how the interviewer prepares her thematisation and questions in advance, and how she behaves during the interview situation. As was discussed in the chapter on interviews, based on the research question, the student, who opts to work with focus groups, prepares an interview or thematic guide that may be more or less structured and comprehensive. The degree to which the guide is structured will have an influence on how active a role the interviewer plays during the actual focus-group interview.

In cases where the student conducts several parallel interviews, she must also decide whether to work with a standardised interview guide, or whether the themes/questions for the groups will vary. The immediate advantage of using a relatively standardised interview guide is that it allows for comparison between groups. Conversely, a guide that allows for variation makes it possible to learn as you go and increases flexibility in relation to pursuing avenues of discussion that are of interest to the individual groups. In this sense, standardisation is linked to structuring, but they are not the same.

Nevertheless, it is important to stress that both structuring and standardisation, regardless of the circumstances, will only be applicable to a certain extent, as the purpose of the focus group will always be to allow participants to steer elements of the discussion without too much intervention from the interviewer. In some cases, of course, it will be appropriate for the interviewer to interrupt—for example, if she considers the discussion to have taken a turn that deviates from the topic. Another reason to intervene could be to make sure that everybody gets the chance to speak, or the interviewer might ask for a more in-depth response or for verbalisation of a non-verbal reaction (for example if a person nods or shakes her head). Although group discussion is key in the focus group, this does not mean that the interviewer must remain passive. Her responsibility is to maintain focus, facilitate fruitful discussion and generate material that is useful in relation to the research question.

As well as providing a means of asking questions, focus groups have a long tradition of being used to present participants with material that they are collectively asked to relate to and discuss. This may, for example, be a television advert, a physical product or examples of management communication. In Merton and Kendall's (1946) introduction of the method into the social sciences, the groups had to relate to and discuss specific films and radio programmes. In a marketing context, too, under both commercial and academic auspices, the interviewer will often present the participants with examples of products that they are asked to discuss in terms of design, usability, and so on. Finally, in more critical organisational studies, there are examples of focus groups being used to study how staff relate to "corporate communication," based on specific examples (Llewellyn & Harrison, 2006).

The focus-group interview typically results in fairly extensive material that it is virtually impossible to retain and use in analysis unless it has been recorded in either video or audio form and the content transcribed. It is therefore worth repeating the relatively simple practical advice that the recording equipment should be checked in advance to make sure that there is enough hard-disk space and the battery is fully charged. Most people agree that the recordings should be transcribed. How accurate the transcripts need to be depends—as is the case for individual interviews—on what they will be used for. If you work with discourse analysis or conversation analysis, for example, it is vital that everything is noted, including interrupted speech, pauses, laughter, and so on (Bloor *et al.*, 2001: 59). Other types of analysis do not necessarily require the transcription to be quite so detailed.

Focus-group interviews can be used as the sole method in a study, but they will usually be combined with other methods, be they qualitative (individual interviews, document studies, observation) or quantitative (surveys) (Eriksson & Kovalainen, 2008: 176).

In relation to the subsequent analysis, it is often a very good idea to work with one or another form of coding to bring some order to what will typically be fairly extensive material. This coding can be more or less formalised and systematised. In addition, the actual analysis of the material depends, to a very high degree, on the research question and perspective. Some researchers, particularly those working in the constructivist and phenomenological traditions, will often replace a systematic coding process with a more "ethnographic" reading (Halkier, 2002).

Perspectives—implications

In a realist perspective, the purpose of the focus group is typically to identify individuals' attitudes, perceptions or points of view—for example, in relation to a new product on the market or the launch of a political campaign. The idea can be to use a small group to test consumer reaction in advance before the product is marketed in its final form. As we have seen in the previous chapters, the realist perspective assumes that individuals are equipped with certain emotions, attitudes and points of view, and that it is the task of the researcher or student to identify and then represent them in her study. Seen from this perspective, the focus-group interview becomes a tool used to bring these otherwise hidden attitudes to light. The more accurately people put forward their actual views, the more effective the interview. As we shall see, this is reflected in the case-study description below, of Carrigan and Attalla's (2001) study of whether companies' ethical profiles affect consumer behaviour.

The focus-group interview method stems from a realist tradition, albeit with elements that are more reminiscent of a phenomenological approach. Merton and his colleagues stressed, therefore, that the focus-group interview could be used to expound on what individuals mean when they say, for example, that a particular propaganda film is "unpleasant" (Merton & Kendall, 1946). On the one hand, therefore, there is a perception that individuals have inherent attitudes, emotions, and so on. This is consistent with the realist perspective. On the other hand, there is also a focus on the individuals' subjective experience and personal interpretation of what it means when something is experienced as unpleasant, and this must be expounded and interpreted in order to be meaningful. This can be said to be closer to the phenomenology perspective.

The vast majority of researchers who use the focus-group interview work within a variant of what this book calls a realist perspective. In practice, this means that here, too, some of the methodological considerations are concerned with trying to reduce the interviewer effect and other aspects that may have an adverse affect on the sought-after objectivity and neutrality.

It is apparently relatively rare for the focus-group method to be used in studies that work directly with a phenomenology perspective. Presumably, this is due mainly to the fact that phenomenology's focus on subjectivity and in-depth insight is more compatible with the individual interview. Due to the form and the multiple participants, it is difficult, in a focus-group interview, to obtain a picture of an individual's life-

Qualitative Research Methods in Organisation Studies

world and the importance that different phenomena assume in relation to it. However, several researchers do refer to the aspect of phenomenology that assigns greater weighting to the intersubjective (e.g., Schutz & Natanson, 1962). As mentioned in the introductory chapter, this aspect of phenomenology has some points of overlap with parts of constructivism. The previously mentioned study by Halkier (2002), of attitudes to food safety among families with young children, is an example of a study that deliberately links a phenomenological and a social-constructivist approach in its focus-group work.

A number of researchers in the constructivist tradition have adopted this method in recent years. Demant (2006) even argues that focus groups are particularly meaningful in the constructivist perspective, the aim of which is to illustrate exactly the kind of complexity emphasised in the group situation. In this perspective it is the social and processual aspects that are interesting, rather than individual attitudes and perceptions. This means that the focus group is more suitable in some contexts than, for example, the personal in-depth interview, because this kind of group interview forms the basis for social interaction and lets it be the key aspect.

Regardless of the perspective with which you work, there is an assumption that what happens in the focus group reflects, in some sense or other, something that also takes place outside of this specific context. Unlike in the realist perspective, the constructivist does *not* assume that the focus group will generate statements that reflect individuals' actual actions or attitudes as they manifest themselves "in reality." Instead, the focus is on how participants in the focus group continuously orient themselves toward the other participants, and in the process attempt to portray themselves in certain ways. Constructivism, then, assumes that the focus group reflects something external and can be used to "re-construct some of the cultural processes that are active [...]" in other contexts (Demant, 2006: 135).

Case study: Marketing

Market research is one of the areas in which focus groups are particularly heavily used. In the following case study, we will describe an example from a study that used focus groups as its primary research tool. Carrigan and Attalla (2001) wanted to study whether corporate ethics have an impact on consumer behaviour. More specifically, they studied whether the knowledge that a particular organisation acts in a morally problematic manner in some context or other leads to the consumer consciously opting out or perhaps even completely boycotting the company. According to the literature in this area, there is a great deal of evidence to suggest that such a link does exist. Carrigan and Attalla used the focus group to test whether this was in fact the case.

The article does not explicitly state its theoretical perspective, but the realist perspective and its basic hypotheses are evident, for example when the authors state that the intention of the focus group was to elicit consumers' thoughts and attitudes in relation to the topic of ethical and unethical behaviour in the market. In other words, there is an assumption that consumers' inherent attitudes toward the topic can be reproduced in the focus-group interview.

The researchers chose to conduct two focus-group interviews (which they refer to as focus-group discussions). There were five people in each group. The authors reflect upon the fact that this number of participants is lower than that usually proposed in the methodology literature, but stress that a relatively low number of participants may be beneficial in situations where the subject is sensitive. In addition, due to the supposed sensitivity of the issue, the researchers divided the participants into two groups, one of women and one of men. This ensured a certain degree of homogeneity. Both sessions were recorded after the researchers had asked for the participants' permission in advance. Prior to the focus groups, a discussion guide had been drawn up. Here is an excerpt from their study.

When asked if they had ever boycotted a product, not one respondent stated that they had. The moderator specifically mentioned Nike, and all but one of the respondents were aware of the publicity surrounding Nike's employment practices in the developing world. However, despite accepting that Nike had a poor ethical record, respondents stated that they would still buy Nike products. [...]

One female respondent said:

"It is exploitation, but without companies such as Nike, they wouldn't have a job at all."

Another said:

"If someone is clever enough to set up a company in this way, earning huge profits, then fair enough." [...]

The moderator introduced the issue of chocolate production to the groups, mentioning the low wages of producers. Although respondents stated they were unhappy at low wages being paid to people producing chocolate for them they said they would still not be willing to boycott products over this issue.

When asked to identify socially responsible firms, all respondents singled out Body Shop, but were quick to point out that they shopped there not to be socially responsible but because they liked the products. [...]

One issue that did engage sympathy from the respondents was animal rights, particularly the idea that animals suffered due to corporate behaviour. [...] This topic did create a lot of debate and it became clear that the respondents only cared about certain kinds of social issues. For example, the rainforest and working conditions were low on their list of ethical priorities, while the idea of animals, and in particular dolphins, being killed or maimed did matter to them enough to affect their purchase behaviour [...]:

"I'd be a lot less inclined to buy if I knew for a fact that companies were harming animals." [...]

When asked what factors most strongly influenced their buying decisions, they concluded that price, value, brand image and fashion trends were the four most important factors. However, as the discussion progressed, they did state that if they were made aware of any unethical or irresponsible corporate behaviour through media exposure, this would affect their purchase decision:

"If it gets a lot of media coverage, then it makes me think twice the next time about what I am buying."

However, another respondent did say:

"We all know about McDonald's cutting down trees and promoting unhealthy food, but all of us here eat McDonald's." [...]

Finally, most participants were keen to point out that if they could financially afford to discriminate against those unethical companies, they would pay the premium for any good quality products that were produced through a more responsible approach.

(Carrigan & Attalla, 2001: 568–570)

As mentioned above, this particular case study is based on a realist perspective. This is particularly evident when you look at how the excerpt is presented and analysed, and how the authors use their analysis of this material to reach a certain type of conclusion. In a realist perspective, there is an assumption that the focus group participants have inherent attitudes, for example, in relation to what determines whether they buy or possibly boycott certain products that are produced under unethical conditions. In other words, the assumption is that these attitudes are already firmly established among the participants *before* the focus group is convened. Individuals are assumed to *hold* certain attitudes and display corresponding behaviour. Through this lens, the focus group is a tool that is particularly well suited to bringing these pre-existing attitudes to light. What is interesting is primarily the individuals' attitudes and actions, not the interaction within the focus group *per se*.

This does not mean that the interaction is considered unimportant, or that the researchers might just as well have conducted individual interviews. Rather, the interaction is seen as an ideal tool for getting people to talk more honestly and express their true attitudes in a way that they might otherwise be reluctant to do if they were sitting across from an interviewer. The logic seems to be that they take note of the fact that the other participants do not refrain from buying products from companies with a poor ethical reputation, and this encourages them to admit openly that they feel the same way. The fact that the focus is primarily on individual attitudes and actions can be seen, for example, in the reporting back of the findings, where single statements from the participants are presented out of context. The reader does not hear what the other participants said ahead of the presented statements, nor do they know what is being reacted to in the highlighted statements.

At the same time, we see in the above excerpt that the collective plays a role in the presentation, but in this context it is primarily seen as the sum of the individual attitudes. It is emphasised repeatedly that the respondents agree that companies' ethical profiles play a very small role in relation to their own actual consumer behaviour. Similarly, it shows that there is consensus that the ethical issue that matters most is animal welfare, while wages and the environment do not play a particularly important role. The authors present these attitudes as *findings*, and conclude that companies' ethics possibly play a smaller role for the users than is often assumed in sales and marketing theory. They use their results to falsify a hypothesis that there is a definite correlation between company ethics and consumer behaviour, which can be viewed as two different variables.

Discussion of the case study from a constructivist perspective
In a constructivist perspective, both the analysis and the conclusion would be different. A constructivist researcher would possibly choose more or less the same group in terms of size and composition, but the purpose—or the problem to be discussed—would be different. The analytical view, too, would be significantly different from that which steers the presentation in the excerpt reproduced here.

Firstly, it would not be assumed that individuals have stable and consistent attitudes to an issue like corporate ethics and questions about how they would act on the basis of knowledge of these ethics. Instead, the constructivist sees attitudes as far more flexible, malleable and context-dependent, and therefore as something that is actively shaped *in* the actual focus group. While the group's seemingly strong agreement is regarded by the realist researcher as factually representative of the individuals' actual attitudes and actions (as they exist independently of the focus group), the constructivist will typically focus on the processes in the focus group that help to *create* this consensus in the specific situation. How is what we might call a "discursive space" established in which we can all declare ourselves in agreement that the killing of dolphins is deeply problematic, while factors such as the underpayment of workers

Qualitative Research Methods in Organisation Studies

are less significant and do not have the same effect on our actions? The constructivist will typically look at the way in which there is a kind of negotiation within the group that determines which attitudes and types of consumer behaviour are considered legitimate. It might be said that while the realist sees the striking consensus among the focus group's participants as a finding that can be used to problematise (or even falsify) a particular theoretical hypothesis—i.e., that there is a link between company ethics and consumer behaviour—the constructivist instead sees the agreement as something that is generated, in a certain way, in the interaction between the focus group's participants. Here, the consensus is not a finding as such (something on which the researcher would report back) but rather something that has to be explained via analysis.

Similarly, some constructivists will focus in particular on how the participants use language to construct a community and a common identity. An interesting example is the statement when one of the participants says that "all of us" in the focus group eat at McDonald's. This person is not only speaking for herself, but on behalf of the whole group.

In relation to Chapter One's discussion of the difference between "what" and "how" questions, this case study illustrates that what is interesting in the realist perspective is *what* participants' report, while the constructivist will focus on *how* agreement is established within the group.

Summary
In this chapter we have presented and discussed focus groups as a particular form of qualitative method that is increasingly used in both realist- and constructivist-inspired studies. We have also seen an example of researchers who combine this method with a more phenomenological approach (Halkier, 2002) but, thus far, this approach is less common. This chapter

has therefore focused less on the phenomenological perspective than the previous chapters. The focus-group method contains elements that are reminiscent of both the interview and the observation study. One advantage of focus groups is that this method allows the respondents to relate to each other instead of, as in the individual interview, only to the interviewer. Regardless of perspective, researchers agree that it is precisely the group dialogue and interaction that is the focus group's strength compared to other methods.

We have also argued that all of the different phases of the student's work with focus groups require careful consideration and conscious reflection on how exactly this method helps to shed light on the chosen problem. Successful focus groups require practical choices to be made. Who participates, how many are involved and what role the interviewer plays—all of these issues must be considered. In addition, we have shown that these conditions—as is the case in relation to the other methods—have different consequences for the planning, implementation and analysis of focus groups. Both practically and theoretically, it makes a difference whether you work with focus groups within a realist, phenomenological or constructivist perspective.

Suggested reading

Robert Merton and Patricia Kendall's (1946) article "The Focused Interview" is the classic text on the focus-group interview. It is not only interesting because it harks back to the very earliest days of the method—it also includes reflections on the potential of the focus group that are still relevant today.

Focus Groups: Theory and practice, by David Stewart, Prem Shamdasani and Dennis Rook (2007), includes in-depth reflections on all of the phases of the focus-group interview. It is therefore particularly relevant during the preparatory phase.

Javier Lezaun's article "A Market of Opinions: The political epistemology of focus groups" (2007) is not an application-oriented article, but adopts a more philosophical approach to the focus group. It offers in-depth critical, epistemological and ontological reflections on the method and its effects. The article is a clear example of a text with a constructivist perspective on focus groups.

Exercises

1) In the case study cited, the two researchers argue that the topic of the discussion is a "sensitive issue" and that the focus groups therefore should not have many participants. They also divide the participants into two distinct groups (men and women). Discuss what issues (relevant to your own study programme) you consider to be potentially sensitive. And do you agree that the topic of this case study is sensitive? Justify your answer.

2) Discuss the advantages/disadvantages of focus groups comprising participants who know each other beforehand. Find an example of a problem where you consider this to be an advantage, and another where you believe it is preferable that the participants do not know each other.

3) Discuss how the focus group can complement other methods in a study, such as interviews and observations. Discuss also whether it is possible to combine focus groups with quantitative methods (e.g., surveys).

4) Formulate a research question for the presented case study based on a constructivist perspective.

5) Discuss the ethical considerations you have to take into account when working with focus groups.

CHAPTER 5

Participant observation

Introduction

Participant observation is often a useful data collection tool. It involves the observer participating in the everyday life (at work) of the people she is studying. This participation allows her to observe what is happening, listen to what is said and pose questions whenever she chooses (Becker & Geer, 1957: 28, quoted in Denscombe, 2007: 217).

In contrast, for example, to the interview method, participant observation enables the student to acquire more informal knowledge about the organisation or object of the study (Myers, 2009: 138, Hammersley & Atkinson, 2002). There are also other significant differences.

First, unlike the interview method, participant observation does not require you to make appointments to meet the people you are studying at a specific time—rather, it can be said to continue for as long as the student remains in the workplace. Second, in contrast to the interview, which typically takes about an hour, observation is a somewhat time-consuming method. (However, cf. Chapter Three, the interview is also time-consuming due to the subsequent stages—transcription, coding, analyses, etc.). Third, participant observation is well suited to building up first-hand, unprocessed knowledge about practice, but not *reported* practice, as is the case with the interview.

One of the major benefits of the participant-observation method is that you can observe real-life, real-time interaction.

This makes it possible to analyse the impact of context on human actions and attitudes, thereby gaining a deeper understanding of the phenomenon studied. Similarly, participant observation provides information about what organisational theory calls "tacit knowledge" (Polanyi, 1966). In other words, it enables the student to spot things that are taken for granted in an organisation to such an extent that participants do not think about them in everyday life and therefore would not mention them in an interview. It is also claimed that participant observation encourages creativity in a study, in that we discover new, surprising things in the field (Patton, 1990).

The student can choose to observe, or to participate *and* observe. She can choose merely to observe the practice unfolding in front of her from an "outside-looking-in" viewpoint. In these observations, she does not actively take part in the activities she is observing. To use a colloquial and slightly clichéd phrase, we might say that the observer attempts to be "a fly on the wall." However, the student can also assume a more active role as participant/observer, seeking knowledge about the practice from an "insider" viewpoint. In such cases, the student is part of the activities she is studying. The challenge is to combine the two positions—participation and observation—so that she both gains the insider's understanding and communicates it to the outsider (Wolcott, 1995; Hammersley & Atkinson, 2002).

The observation role is an extension of classic studies in social psychology in which researchers, for example, systematically observed interaction between pupils and between pupils and teachers (Simon & Boyer, 1970). This type of study was, and is, often very quantitative in its design and approach. For example, time studies are made of who speaks and how long different people hold the floor in various meeting forums. Body language is also closely observed and noted, using a checklist. As such, systematic observation studies have similarities with techniques developed in the natural sciences, where quantification is key. This approach is therefore closely associated with a more positivist or realist perspective.

Participant observation in Western society took off in Chicago during the 1920s and 1930s. During this period, a number of studies looking at crime, deviation, race issues, and so on in urban areas were conducted using the participant-observation method. For example, the sociologist Robert Park told his students to study the rapid urbanisation of the city by venturing forth, taking part and observing the consequences (May, 2001: 147ff).

Although observation studies were not a new method of scientific study, social science *participant*-observation studies were different. In contrast to positivist-inspired observation studies (e.g., Croll, 1986), a social research approach is often informed by a phenomenological perspective. Taking this departure, the objective is to gain insight into the life-world being observed by taking part in the activities of the people being studied. In this chapter, we have chosen to focus primarily on the participant-observation method, as it is the most commonly chosen type of observation method.

The method has also increasingly gained ground in organisational studies. Some researchers have studied how, in certain work situations, organisational members create meaning from their everyday activities (Kunda, 1992; Watson, 1994). Others have used participant observation to examine gender and power in organisations (Alvesson, 1998). Typically, participant-observation studies of organisational issues are far shorter than the traditional 6–12-month anthropological studies (often called fieldwork because of their duration).

Concepts, key questions and theory

Concepts such as unpredictability and creativity are often associated with the participant-observation method. Indeed, this qualitative method can be quite far removed from a linear process in which the student seeks to plan her research in detail. Nevertheless, the method still has to be closely linked to the purpose of the study and the research question. If the student does not know what to look out for—and ask about in the organisation's canteen—she may end up spending her time taking notes on events that later prove useless in relation to her research questions and chosen area of analysis.

As with the interview and focus groups, participant observation can be more or less structured depending on whether the student draws up a structured, standardised observation guide and follows it in practice. A student may not have time for a long period of anthropological fieldwork to study and explore an organisational field in a less focused manner. Instead, she may only have a couple of days, or at most a week, so there may well be good reasons to make her observation very focused and relatively structured. One way of focusing participant observation is to base it on a particular thematic focal point. For example, in their study of safety on a building site, Gheradi and Nicolini (2002) concentrated on the learning mechanisms associated with the workers familiarising themselves with safe practices in the workplace. They took note of incidents, interaction and conversations related to this particular theme. Gheradi and Nicolini also further narrowed their focus by "shadowing" one particular worker for the three months that the fieldwork lasted.

Other studies use participant observation as a kind of pilot study, the purpose of which is to learn more about the phenomenon being studied. This in turn makes it possible to decide upon a focus for the study's research question, interview guide, etc. In this context, the days spent in an organisation (for example) serve solely as inspiration, and so the notes only need to help the researcher remember themes and so on. In other words, they will not be used as empirical data in the study, and will not form part of the basis for the analysis either.

There can be (and are) many good reasons for students to use the participant-observation method in exactly this way, as it can help to ensure that the study is relevant to the actors involved. In other words, it helps students to avoid spending unnecessary time preparing research questions, interview questions, etc. that later prove to be irrelevant to the people involved. In this chapter, however, we will discuss the participant-observation method on the basis of the assumption that the student will use her observations to generate knowledge that will be included as empirical material in the study, in the form of field notes (i.e., notes made during her participant observations).

The main objective behind choosing the participant-observation method is, as mentioned previously, to gain some kind of "inside" knowledge of the problem. The purpose of spending days, weeks or, in some cases, months in an organisation is to talk to and observe people in their natural settings (Denscombe, 2007: 217). The student may opt for one of several different roles: the total participant; the participant as observer; the observer as participant; and the total observer (Gold, 1969). This is a continuum, the two extremes of which—the total participant (in anthropology, also known as "going native," cf. Denscombe, 2007: 222) and the total observer—will often not be particularly useful roles in a shorter, more exploratory study. The total participant is a time-consuming role, since the assumption is that total participation (in some cases, undercover) has to cover a prolonged period if the knowledge generated is to be worthwhile. As mentioned above, the total observer is a role and technique that can be used for more quantitative measurements of human actions.

The role of participant-as-observer is conducted by the student who tells everybody openly about both her project and the purpose of her presence. She does not participate fully, but maintains a distance to the practice. The observer-as-participant role is conducted by the student who has very little time at her disposal, and is therefore able to establish only short time-relations with the people covered by the study. This role is also based on an open and honest relationship with those people (May, 2001: 154ff). Gold (1969: 36ff) clarifies that the observer as participant—because of the time restraints that define the role—risks misunderstanding things during her period of observation. For this reason, she should supplement her observations with other methods of data collection.

Regardless of whether you adopt the role of participant as observer or observer as participant, it might be said that the student and her interpretations constitute the actual study tools in this method (Denscombe, 2007: 221; Esterberg 2002: 61ff). If you work within this perspective, therefore, you may wish, for example, to test and review your observation notes by consulting the people involved (respondent validation) (Kvale, 1996). This is not a matter of the actors having to approve analyses, but rather of affording them the opportunity to discuss the *observations* with the student and eliminate any potential misunderstandings.

As is the case for interviews and focus groups, it is important to consider how your observations will be stored in a form that allows for subsequent analysis. When observations are conducted over a very short period of time—typically meetings of one kind or another—it is often a good idea to make audio or video recordings for subsequent transcription. It is, of course, a prerequisite that you obtain permission to record the participants, which is not always possible. In participant-observation studies where you spend whole days in a particular environment and take part in the general day-to-day activities, audio and video recordings are not really a practical option, and the student must record her observations by taking careful notes.

In participant observation, developing well thought-out techniques for writing field notes will help to ensure the quality of your study (Emerson *et al.*, 1995). Many researchers point out that it is important: 1) that you take notes in the field rather than writing them down when you get home; 2) that they are very detailed; and 3) that they seek to separate (objective) descriptions from (subjective) evaluations of what you have observed. Although this distinction between objective descriptions and subjective evaluations can be said to stem from a realist perspective, which makes a sharp distinction between reality and interpretation, the distinction can also be applied as a pragmatic technique in the phenomenological and constructivist perspectives. This is to do with the fact that, regardless of perspective, it is difficult to analyse heavily interpreted notes, as they have a tendency to stop you spotting new links in your material.

It is therefore important—regardless of perspective—to decide what type of notes to take to distinguish between the different types. Four types of notes are commonly used: 1) brief notes, the purpose of which is to act as a reminder of an event; 2) descriptive notes, the purpose of which is to reproduce an event in as detailed a manner as possible; 3) analytical notes, the purpose of which is to relate the descriptive notes to each other (the first stage of an analysis); and 4) reflective notes, the purpose of which is to document your feelings, your thoughts and the knowledge you have acquired in the field (Eriksson & Kovalainen, 2008: 148). And finally, as mentioned at the beginning of this chapter, it is very important that you observe (and note) events and actions that are related to the problem being studied.

When using observation notes later in a study, a variety of techniques are at your disposal. As a rule, notes will be good for contextualising the study; for example, writing a rich introduction will be important for the reader. Notes can also be used to underpin analyses based on, for example, interviews, focus groups or document material. You may have noted the same as, or the opposite of, what was found using other methods, for instance. In both cases, your observations can be used as an instrument of reflection in the analysis. If it is sufficiently rich in detail and does not contain too many assessments and evaluations, participant-observation material can also be used as raw data; you can write up a meeting and subsequently analyse the description in the same way as you would analyse any other document.

As mentioned previously, the participant-observation method has a number of advantages. In technical terms, it is an easy method of gaining insider knowledge and insight into the context. Denscombe (2007: 224) also argues that, because of its context-sensitivity, this method is particularly well placed to produce "holistic" analyses. However, the method also has a number of disadvantages. It is time-consuming—both to start and to implement—and it is not always easy to obtain access. As it is a highly subjective method, in which the student is her own tool, there is also an increased risk of misunderstanding and, therefore, misinterpretation (Denscombe, 2007: 225). In a realist perspective, it is possible to criticise studies based on participant observation on the basis that they have a low level of reliability.

Participant observation requires informed consent from the organisation and from the actors the student encounters in her work. Although the research includes some well-known examples of participant observers who have gone undercover to make their observations, it must be stressed that, as a general rule, this is unethical, and students should always inform the actors that they are being observed. It is a good idea to consider whether to offer anonymity—and if so, how this might be achieved. Before the participant observation commences, it is also recommended that students outline in writing what the project is about, in which publications the results are likely to appear, and so on.

Below, we will consider the implications of the three different perspectives—realism, phenomenology and constructivism—for the participant-observation method.

Perspectives—implications

The roots of observation studies can be traced back to positivist-inspired studies that focus on the measurement of behaviour, while participant-observation studies can be traced back to anthropological studies of "exotic" cultures in the early 20th century (for example the anthropologist Malinowski's studies in Melanesia in the 1920s) and to Western sociological studies of classic themes such as poverty and crime. We are dealing here with a method that has clear phenomenological features due to its relation to traditional social research studies of human actions and their underlying motives. It is worth noting that these studies are often born of a desire to understand a social phenomenon from the studied actors' perspective (their life-world). Anthropology uses the concept "emic" for this "from-the-inside" understanding, in contrast to the "etic" observer—the "outsider's" perspective (Hedland, 1990).

In more realist-inspired studies, there is a tendency to develop methods and techniques to ensure that the student's personal situation (gender, age, educational background, etc.)

plays as small a role as possible. Due to the ideal of capturing an objective reality, the most useful material in this perspective will be that which is collected by means of pure observation methods, for example based on templates.

In phenomenology-inspired studies, on the other hand, the student will try to capture the actors' life-worlds in a tangible and methodical manner by establishing a trusting and empathetic relationship with them. The aim is, through empathy and sensitivity, to get as close as possible to their everyday lives and experiences. The goal is to gain insight into the collective world in relation to which their actions should be understood. The student should intervene as little as possible in order to minimise her impact upon the site being studied.

In constructivist-inspired studies, the starting point for participant observation is that the student will influence the field via her personality, experiences and research focus. However, the assumption is that this effect is an inherent condition of social science studies that emphasise the importance of human activity. In constructivist studies, the student will not, therefore, try to minimise her impact on the actors in the field, but instead actively relate to these basic conditions in her analysis work.

Realism

An important objective of the realist-inspired study is to get "behind the façade" of, for example, the organisation being studied. One important reason to conduct observation studies in which the student personally documents practice is to avoid the sources of error that, for the student inspired by realism, will necessarily be present in the majority of qualitative studies that use, for example, the interview method (reported practice). Another important reason is to gain an insight into the reality—or, rather, Reality—that remains concealed when an organisation, for example, talks about women and management on its website or in an interview situation. Realism's "depth" metaphor is well suited to understanding what drives the realist-inspired researcher out in the field: she needs to get behind the façade and go below the surface to gain an insight into what is *really* happening in the organisation. The aim is to coax out an undistorted picture of the organisation's practice, one that has not been mediated through subjective interview narratives. The realism-inspired student thus seeks to reveal the "world out there" (as it really is).

Phenomenology

Since phenomenology, as mentioned earlier, is the perspective best suited to the participant-observation method, it is hardly surprising that it is the perspective most frequently used in participant-observation studies (Ybema, *et al.*, 2009; Hammersley & Atkinson, 2002). Phenomenology's ambition of gaining insight into the life-world of the actors requires sensitivity and empathy on the part of the student. Participant observation carried out over a longer period is assumed to be the method best suited to ensuring the empathy that is a precondition for understanding the participants' everyday lives and collective world.

These studies wish to produce "emic"—insider—knowledge, which illustrates the underlying purpose of phenomenology-inspired participant observation. The student has to engender an "insider" view with the field's actors in order to understand their everyday existence and life-worlds from the inside (Ybema *et al.*, 2009). The focus is on the participants' experiences and feelings and the motives for their actions. The assumption is that you can analyse your way to these experiences, feelings and motives if you are sufficiently intimate with the actors. The "emic" knowledge must then continuously be challenged by the "etic" knowledge. In other words, there is an ongoing interaction between participation (the insider's view) and observation (the outsider's view). Optimally, the student starts her participant observation without any preconceived notions. If she has decided on a theory in advance, it must be put to the side so it does not preclude a deeper understanding stemming from the collective experiences she will share with the actors in the field.

The student inspired by phenomenology will seek "objectively produced descriptions of subjectively produced opinions" (Järvinen & Mik-Meyer, 2005: 104). The student therefore seeks to understand "the world in there" (in the participant). Just as the student who adopts a realist perspective tries to describe "the world out there," the phenomenologist attempts to gain insight into a reality that may remain hidden if the student relies solely on interviews and document analysis.

Constructivism

In constructivist studies that make use of participant observation, the idea is not to gain knowledge of the actors' experiences, feelings and motives for their actions in order to achieve an understanding of the world as the actors experience it. The constructivist perspective does emphasise the relationships between social actors but, in contrast to phenomenology, the constructivist perspective has no ambition of understanding reality as understood by the participants. The student who adopts a constructivist perspective can describe experiences from the field that are based on collective participation in activities, but these experiences remain the student's own. Unlike the phenomenologist, the constructivist is not interested in reaching an understanding of subjective meaning, experiences and motives. The focus is unambiguously on the *relations* between the participating actors, and any attempt to understand the actors "from the inside" will constitute a break with the perspective. This means that, in the constructivist perspective, the participant-observer typically focuses on practices and institutional conditions. In other words, the attention is "automatically [...] away from individuals' 'private experiences,' and [the observer] directs attention instead to how the subjects (inter)act, and how the social context—both specific and more general—affects this interaction" (Järvinen & Mik-Meyer, 2005: 97).

In contrast to the phenomenology perspective, which seeks to approach the study without theory, the constructivist-inspired researcher will actively relate to theory in advance of her participant observations. The theory is not therefore regarded as a deterrent to understanding the world seen from the inside, but rather is understood as qualifying a viewpoint that could never be neutral, free from theory or unbiased.

The assumption is that the research design, choice of organisation for the case study, choice of problem, focus for the participant observation, interview questions, and so on, are all defined in the theory upon which the project will draw.

Case study: Corporate social responsibility (CSR)

Participant observation is a method that is increasingly used in organisational research. In the case study we have chosen to illustrate the method, Roepstorff (2010) used participant observation, research interviews and analysis to learn how the company IKEA approached corporate social responsibility (CSR). The study was for a PhD project, so time was available for prolonged observation. In this case, we have chosen a form of presentation that uses both excerpts from Roepstorff's book and our analyses of those extracts. Indented text in quotation marks indicates a quote from the book. Text without quotation marks signifies our analyses of the quotations.

"The idea of the book, as mentioned, is to follow the intention and the concept of Corporate Social Responsibility (CSR) from the political and agitational context to daily practice in companies. One aspect concerns what the originators of the concept, the Ministry of Social Affairs and the government of the day, considered to be the intention and content of the concept. Another is how it is perceived, used and practised where it is supposed to be implemented, in companies" (Roepstorff, 2010: 18).

This description of the purpose—which can be read as a way of communicating the research question—justifies the participant-observation method. Roepstorff does not want merely to consider the political intentions behind CSR. She wants to focus closely on how CSR is "perceived, used and practised" in the companies that work with it. Roepstorff herself clarifies this point in the following quote and, at the same time, positions the project within the constructivist/phenomenological traditions:

"In this way, the analytical angle of the study of CSR in this book therefore also has an impact on the methodological approach, and of course the problem. In this context, the aim is to try to reveal how companies relate to the idea of CSR not just with words (conceptually), but also through actions (practice). The problem suggests that neither the concept nor the actions are defined in advance, but that *the definitions* and *how* to act 'socially responsibly' are at the very heart of what is being studied" (Roepstorff, 2010: 19—author's own emphasis).

As she puts it, the analytical angle, the methodological approach and the problem are all linked together. She then looks at definitions and poses a "how" question that has to be answered by using both concepts (theory) and the knowledge of practice that she has gained through participant observation. As Roepstorff shows here, and as we have argued several times in this book, the choice of research question should shape the choice of method and analytical angle (theory). Her choice to explore the actual process of definition, during which meaning is attributed to "CSR" in practice, and her highlighting of the fact that she bases this on a "how" approach (with focus on the process of the development of CSR), positions the study in a constructivist and/or phenomenological perspective. Had the project been informed by a realist perspective, the exercise would have been different. In that case, she might instead have studied *what* CSR is, and whether the company has, in fact, implemented "real" CSR. The assumption would have been that the concept has an essential meaning that can be defined in advance. Moreover, it would have been natural to look at which actors actually work with CSR, and why some companies have more or less success in their work with CSR (the nature of which would be clearly defined). Perhaps we can get a bit closer to Roepstorff's somewhat different perspective:

> "To examine CSR in Danish reality or everyday life, the researcher needs to obtain a complex and thorough insight into this reality or everyday life. [...] In this context, participant observation is practised in a single company. [...] Participant observation is, in this way, used to get behind the façade of talk of social responsibility and gain an impression of the various cultural positions and practices that exist internally in the company. This challenges, once

again, an essentialist understanding of culture" (Roepstorff, 2010: 19).

On the one hand, the author wants to "get behind the façade of talk" about social responsibility, which on the face of it pulls the project more in a phenomenological direction (because of the depth metaphor implied by getting "behind" to look at everyday practice). On the other hand, her aim is for the project to challenge an essentialist understanding of culture, which is indicative of a prototypical constructivist project. The introduction to the book brings us no closer to the perspective, so let us turn instead to the practical methodological considerations Roepstorff made prior to her participant observation, and the way in which she gains access to the field:

"My nerves are jangling a bit. It's Monday, 4 March 2002. For a few months, I've been talking to IKEA about the possibility of doing fieldwork there. The managing director has said OK, the HR boss has said OK. Now all I need is permission from the boss of the store. Today is a rather special day for IKEA. Seven new members of staff are starting work. Most of them are part of a project they are calling the High Potential Programme. The seven have been selected and start an introductory course this morning. I really hope I'll be allowed to take part. [...] I don't have an agreement, or authorisation, but I hope that I can manage to catch the store boss before the course starts, and if I'm really lucky, he'll let me in" (Roepstorff, 2010: 78).

This quote is an example of what, earlier in the chapter, we called reflexive field notes—where the researcher or student takes note of what she has felt, thought, and so on, in the field. Roepstorff was indeed allowed in and attended the introductory course, which marked the start of her prolonged participant observation of IKEA. We have chosen to include the above extract because it very clearly describes the extensive work that can lie behind—and the unpredictability that is often linked to—gaining *access* to the field. In this case, one of the prerequisites is acceptance from three key actors: the managing director, the head of HR and the store manager. As the extract illustrates, in this case it proved necessary to contact all three, each of whom had to be informed about the project before granting approval. Drawing up a one-page text that clarifies the scope of the participant observation, outlines the purpose of the project and contains information regarding anonymity, ethical considerations and so on, can be beneficial if, like Roepstorff, you need the green light from more than one person.

Below, we quote another extract showing how Roepstorff's thinking about methods may help to shed light on the problem:

"During the 3–4 months of full-time field work at IKEA, and my further many months associated with the company, I sought high and low for descriptions, definitions, discussions, understandings, impressions of, and work with, social responsibility. The object of the study was the whole of the IKEA Group's work on social responsibility. The specific elaboration and implementation of the social aspect was followed at international, national and local levels, as well as by looking at the discrepancy and/or correlation between attitude and action at each of these levels" (Roepstorff, 2010: 80).

Here, Roepstorff provides a very telling description of both the advantages and disadvantages of participant observation when she describes the great volume of knowledge (data) that is potentially available to those who employ this method. The advantage is that, like Roepstorff, you shed light on many different aspects of a problem that relates to a complex phenomenon (Roepstorff seeks "high and low" at "international, national and local level"). The embedded exploratory element of participant observation provides the researcher or student with insight into (too) much material. The disadvantage, therefore, is that if the researcher or student does not delineate her problem and the focus of the observations in a way that corresponds to the time available for data collection, she also risks acquiring unfocused data that will result in too much material, which it will be both difficult and time-consuming to process.

Finally, we present an extract from the last page of the book. Here, the author talks about her findings and again justifies (indirectly) her choice of participant observation:

"Individual companies do not just create their way of understanding and acting in a socially responsible manner via the way in which they opt to practice CSR, they also define the space the company has for action and thus the company itself. To be concise: CSR is not just defined and shaped by the company. It seems that *CSR actually defines and shapes the company*" (Roepstorff, 2010: 368—author's own emphasis).

We see here how the choice of methodology exerts a direct influence on the knowledge the study is able to generate. Participant-observation studies allow the researcher to gain insight into processes. This enables her to conclude that CSR as a strategy helps shape the company, and is not therefore merely a neutral tool that the individual company can take down from the shelf and use to whatever degree it wishes. CSR helps to shape and define the company, therefore the strategy has an embedded potential for action, as identified by the researcher through her studies of practice. A study that was either based solely on what was written about CSR (document analysis) or what is said about CSR (interviews, focus groups) would have found it more difficult to analyse its way to this conclusion. Thus, the choice of research method not only has practical consequences, but can also have consequences for the type of knowledge a study is able to produce.

Summary

In this chapter, we have outlined and discussed a number of conditions upon which it may be significant to reflect if you choose to work with the participant-observation method. Our case study was based on a phenomenology/constructivism-inspired approach, but that does not mean that students cannot use the method in a study inspired by realism. In such cases, the problem's purpose will typically be more concerned with *revealing*, and the purpose of participant observation will be to prioritise knowledge that can be used to "explain" and identify causality, for example, between management initiatives and the successful implementation of CSR.

In our presentation of the CSR case study, we used text excerpts that showed how the problem, analytical approach (theory) and choice of method must be seen as three interconnected entities. The reason we have chosen to focus so much on this interconnection is that the participant-observation method's strong exploratory element means that it also entails an inherent risk—namely, that the researcher or student can easily stray onto the wrong track and collect and produce too much data if she does not, from the start, clarify her focus and relate this to practical methodological choices (the focus of her observations).

We have also chosen text excerpts that show that the method can also potentially be very time-consuming. By this, we refer not only to the time the student will need to spend in the field, but also to the time it takes to gain access to the field. Many textbooks also recommend, therefore, that very early in the process—in fact, as soon as you have chosen the organisation—you establish contact and ask permission to carry out participant observation. Furthermore, since the problem may have tangible consequences in terms of methodology (as in Roepstorff's case), it is important to request access early in the process, so that you can adjust your research question in cases where you are not granted permission for participant observation.

Finally, we have chosen text excerpts that show how a study's findings can also be related directly to the researcher or student's choice of methodology. It cannot be overstated that methodological choices are about much more than just drawing up an interview guide and defining focus points for observations. Methodological choices have consequences for what you are able to study and what kind of knowledge you are able to generate.

Suggested reading

Organizational Ethnography: Studying the complexity of every-day life (2009) by Sierk Ybema *et al.* discusses fieldwork in an organisational frame. Many important topics are discussed in the book, for example, the relation between the researcher and her "object of study," "problems of distance and closeness," "the doing of ethnography 'at home,'" etc.

Ethnography: Principles in practice (2002) by Hammersley and Atkinson is a classic text on how to conduct ethnography. The book covers themes such as how to gain access to the field, how to form relations in the field, how to gain insider accounts, and how to organise and analyse your data and write up your analysis.

Exercises

1) Formulate a research question for which participant observation is very much the appropriate method. Justify your answer.

2) Discuss how interviews and participant observation can complement each other. What types of data can participant observation generate that may not be elicited from an interview?

3) Discuss how you would guarantee that your observations would be sufficiently focused if you were to examine CSR practice in an organisation.

4) Discuss how the principle of transparency, as presented in Chapter Two, can be used in connection with participant observation.

5) Discuss the ethical considerations related to participant observation and why there is broad academic agreement that "undercover" observation is unethical.

CHAPTER 6

Documents

Introduction

While the literature about qualitative methodology generally
focuses quite closely on interviews and observations, far fewer
discussions about methodology revolve around how document studies, as a specific form of material, can contribute
to empirical studies (Mik-Meyer, 2005: 193). However, there
are several good reasons to be aware that texts are a useful
form of qualitative material. In particular, when it comes to
organisation studies, it may be highly relevant for the student
to draw on documents in her analysis, for example, because
documents play a crucial role in organisations' actions and
decisions.

Back in the 1920s, Max Weber (2005: 74) stressed that documentation is one of the significant characteristic aspects of
the archetypal bureaucratic form of organisation. Although in
recent years there has been much talk of de-bureaucratisation,
there are clear signs that the need for documentation and production of diverse written statements has not diminished—
quite the contrary, in fact. This trend has been noticed in both
the public and private sectors. Atkinson and Coffey (2004)
assert that documents are an integral part of contemporary
organisational reality.

The majority of social science research, including those
in the field of organisation, also include, to some extent, different types of documents as part of their empirical material.
In this chapter, we will concentrate on the question of what

the student has to think about if she opts to use this form of qualitative material. As in the previous three chapters, we will argue that these reflections and choices ought to be closely related to the study's problem and perspective, and that choices in relation to both selection and analysis vary depending on whether you are working from a realist, phenomenological or constructivist perspective.

Concepts, key questions and theory

In contrast to interviews, focus groups and participant observation, documents exist prior to the study of which they become a part. However, this is not synonymous with the data being more objective or neutral. A document can be defined as data that consists of words and/or images that have become recorded without intervention from a researcher (Silverman, 2001: 119).

Document studies are based on empirical material, which is *material* in the literal sense, even though for the constructivist it has neither an inherent essence nor an unambiguous meaning. Documents are also, in a very literal sense, material that is available in tangible form. This distinguishes them from more elusive objects of analysis, such as individuals' "experiences" or "motives." Silverman's definition also underlines that, in contrast to, for example, the interview, documents are created independently of the researcher's project.

Documents typically contain text, but often also numbers and various forms of visualisation, such as photographs, graphs and diagrams. In this chapter, we will focus primarily on text documents. Other methodology books contain chapters on document studies based on texts that mainly consist of numbers and calculations, such as financial accounts (Pietras-Jensen, 2007a). Others discuss visual material, such as photographs, illustrations and films (Harper, 2002). Particularly within the organisational-theory branch of research into accounting and financial management, there is increased interest in how images are used in annual reports (Davison, 2007). Understandably, studies of sales and marketing have always focused on images and film as empirical material.

In organisation studies, many different types of document can potentially be relevant in relation to the problem. When students write empirically based assignments, documents will almost always, to some extent, be included as a part of the material. The material may consist of documents produced by the organisation itself, such as websites, annual reports, budgets, corporate social responsibility reports, company policies, job adverts, marketing material, press releases and strategies. In other cases, the relevant material may be documents that refer to a particular organisation or a course of events in which the organisation has been involved, for example media articles about a company's level of social responsibility or alleged lack thereof. The relevant texts can also be documents that are not specifically related to a particular organisation, but rather to a certain area or subject with relevance for the organisation or sector that is the empirical pivotal point of the study. Legislation in a particular area is an example of this, for example legislation on the environment, annual reports or EU directives. Finally, there are documents that may have a more informal and unofficial nature than those previously mentioned, such as internal memoranda or drafts.

Some students who use documents in their studies forget to take into account that using these forms of data also requires them to think about methodology, just as interviews or participant observation material do. As mentioned above, the research and methodology literature shows, to some extent, that there have been fewer methodological discussions about this type of material than about the other qualitative methods, such as interviews and observation studies (Mik-Meyer, 2005).

There may be many reasons why the researcher or student chooses to use documents as empirical material in her study. In some cases, part of the research question may involve studying how a given document is produced. Justesen (2008), for example, examines how the Danish National Audit Office's reports are the result of a process that often extends over more than a year and involves a large number of different actors, all of whom, to some extent, can be seen as co-authors of the document, which ultimately appears as a single text. We will return to this later, as it forms the case analysis in this chapter. Companies generally have a number of key texts—for example budgets (Czarniawska-Joerges 1992)—that can be seen as the result of collective writing processes. Along the way, these involve negotiations and interpretations, and sometimes conflicts and struggles, all of which determine the content of the final text.

Other studies focus on how different standards and a mixture of formal and informal rules about genre play a crucial role in determining the form a document will ultimately take. Many of documents in organisations are produced on the basis of an agreed standard (Mik-Meyer & Justesen, 2010: 286), and it can be interesting to illustrate this in an empirical analysis. For example, Van Maanen and Pentland (1994) show how accountants systematically "cleanse" their texts of traces of the uncertainty, ambiguity and subjectivity that characterise the process of document production. The result is a document that hides the writer (with phrases such as "the study has shown that ..." instead of "XX has shown that ...") and generally adopt a style that is technical, dry and clinically cleansed of any kind of pathos (see Justesen & Skærbæk,

2005).

Some studies in organisational theory—in particular, those inspired by the neo-institutional perspective (for example Meyer & Rowan, 1977)—have argued that organisations actively produce and use documents with a view to appearing legitimate to the outside world. The production of a series of documents is therefore connected to a desire to demonstrate rationality, accountability or one of the other values prevalent in the organisation's institutional environment. Goffman's (1959) concept of *impression management* is relevant in this context (Van Maanen & Pentland, 1994).

It might be said that these types of studies focus on documents' *production processes*. Analysis of these processes can, for example, be used to study power relationships within an organisation. Other studies direct their attention instead toward what can be called *the consumption process* (Prior, 2003). Here, the researcher or student uses document material to follow what happens when a document is read and, in particular, when it is *used* in new social contexts that are separate from the document's production process. Justesen (2005), for example, studies how news media and politicians "translate" the National Audit Office's reports and use them to legitimise actions like budget cuts.

Most of the studies that analyse documents' consumption processes do not consider receiving a text to be a purely passive process. Instead, the focus is on how people do different things *with* documents (Prior, 2003). Constructivist studies that are directly inspired by the actor-network theory (e.g., Latour, 1987) even operate with a premise that documents actively do something when they circulate in new contexts (Cooren, 2004).

Finally, there are document studies that look at neither the production nor the consumption process, but instead focus solely on the texts themselves. Here, the focus is directed at the documents' content, style or structure, which is analysed separately from both the production process and how the documents are subsequently received/used by others. This approach is most likely to be seen in a realist perspective, in which the researcher or student will often conduct a form of content analysis (Pietras-Jensen, 2007b). Discourse-theory and semiotic variants of constructivism will also focus on the texts' meaning and discursive aspects.

The concept of *intertextuality* is key in relation to document studies (Atkinson & Coffey, 2004). Intertextuality points to the fact that texts very often refer to other texts. This means that the analysis will, in most cases, relate to a network of documents rather than look at the individual texts as isolated entities. This is especially true of the above-mentioned discourse analyses.

The concept of *genre* often plays a role in document studies as well, during both the selection process and the analysis. The term relates to a relatively homogeneous group of texts that differ from other groups of texts with respect to *style, compositional structure* and *theme* (Bakhtin, 1986: 64).

In addition to more theoretical reflections on how documents are seen and why they are used in a given study, a series of practical questions arises for the student who wants to include document material in her project—just as it does in the case of interviews, participant observations or focus groups. It is important to emphasise again that, just as the considerations about documents outlined above are closely linked to the theoretical perspective and the problem being studied, the answers to the more practical questions are also linked to the overall objective and approach of the study—and are therefore not divorced from theoretical considerations.

The first practical question is which—and how much—

document material to study. How will you select and delineate the relevant text material? What types of texts should be included? What are the criteria for the selection of documents? In purely practical terms, how and where will you search for and find usable documents? To what extent and in what ways can the document-study method be combined with other qualitative or quantitative methods? How will you approach the analysis of the documents?

The question of selection is always important in this context—it makes no sense to say that we have read and used "all" relevant documents. Any study will involve a degree of delineation. It is therefore important to reflect on how the boundaries are drawn, and which criteria are applied in selecting the texts that end up being included as empirical material. As we saw in Chapter Two, the explication of these choices and the reasons for them is inextricably linked with the transparency criterion, which transcends the various theoretical perspectives.

In purely practical terms, it is important to know how you will gain access to relevant documents. Many documents are publicly available, and the Internet has made it easy to find a wealth of potentially relevant texts in a very short time. Most companies make texts available on their own websites, which typically contain direct links to a large number of internally generated documents, such as organisational diagrams, annual reports and CSR reports.

If you are interested in how the media has covered a particular case or organisation, the various newspaper databases may be a suitable tool, as these allow systematic searches of newspapers and periodicals. In addition to publicly available documents, in some cases it is relevant to involve texts that are intended for internal use in the organisation. In studies that relate to the public sector, there is often a large corpus of material that is publicly available. In some cases access may be limited, for example, because the documents contain personal information. At other times, access may be dependent on seeking permission from your contact in order to read and use internal documents. In these cases, you ought to observe the same ethical considerations as you would for interviews and focus groups. In other words, it is important to agree on how you will use the material in question, and the extent to which it may have to be made anonymous.

Perspectives—implications

When it comes to the use of documents as a qualitative method, formulating the study's research question is important, as is its theoretical perspective.

Realism

In a realist perspective, documents will typically be seen as a form of source material that provides the researcher with insight into certain conditions in the world as they are *per se*, i.e., independent of both the research process and the context of the document's origins. The researcher or student sees the reading of documents as a tool that provides access to reality. In this perspective, a document is ideally a kind of transparent medium that neutrally reflects certain circumstances or courses of events in the world that are assumed to exist in a particular way, independently of the research process. Against this background, documents can, for example, be used to try to verify or falsify a given hypothesis (Mik-Meyer & Justesen, 2010: 284). Even though the realist perspective is based on the ontological premise that reality—and therefore the object of analysis—has a particular form prior to the study, the researcher who adopts a realist perspective is aware that documents can refer to several different aspects of reality.

Even the word *document* can, in a certain sense, be said to underpin a realist perception, precisely because it indicates that the text *documents* something or other outside of the text itself. For this reason, some constructivists will be critical of this term, preferring instead to speak of *texts*.

The realist perspective also has a number of consequences in relation to both selection criteria and analysis. Precisely because the student inspired by realism often uses documents as a form of evidence that reflects, for example, organisational or financial conditions in a particular organisation, it is crucial to be "critical" and to choose documents that have a high degree of credibility, neutrality and representativeness. In the realist perspective, analyses will often use documents as evidence that either underpins or undermines a particular hypothesis about certain conditions as they exist in reality. This type of study does not necessarily actually embark on real document analysis, but takes the material and what it says for granted, provided that the data is chosen in a way that guarantees its credibility and representativeness.

Other analyses in this perspective conduct an in-depth *content analysis* of the material itself. This form of analysis tends to approximate a quantitative approach when the researcher, based on systematic coding, measures aspects such as frequency (for example, how frequently a particular word or theme is used) (Pietras-Jensen, 2007b: 61). A related method of analysis is the *template method*, whereby the researcher systematically searches for themes in the text material, but combines this with a more interpretative reading of the texts (ibid.: 63).

Phenomenology
The phenomenology perspective looks differently at both text selection and the analysis of the documents included in a study as empirical material. Here, interpretation is never sim-

ply secondary, but a precondition for all stages of the study. The phenomenology-inspired researcher will often be more interested in "everyday texts" than in polished and official organisation documents, because the perspective typically focuses on everyday organisational life and the actors' (inter) subjective experience of it.

To the extent that official documents are included, the aim of the analysis is typically to study how these documents become meaningful in a person's subjective experience. In other words, the texts are not looked at in relation to an *objective* reality (about which they are assumed to say something) but to a *subjective* world, in which actors interpret and use certain documents in a particular way that is meaningful in relation to the particular life-world of which they are a part. When the researcher who adopts a phenomenological perspective selects her document material, the extent to which it is representative of, or objectively reflects, organisational reality is less crucial. Instead, she will often choose texts that, for one reason or another, are particularly meaningful to the actors who relate to and, in different ways, interpret the documents.

In practice, this often means that, in her study, the researcher or student will combine document studies with interviews and participant observation, because the most important aspect is to analyse *how* subjects perceive, interpret and use documents, and not *what* these documents in themselves say, or do not say, something about. In conclusion, it can be said that the phenomenology-inspired researcher approaches her analysis of the documents *in* their context in a more interpretative manner, and acknowledges that she herself is an interpreter of the material she uses in her study.

Constructivism
The constructivist perspective on document studies differs

from both the realist and the phenomenological perspectives, even though, again, there are overlaps between phenomenology and parts of constructivism. Like the researcher who adopts the phenomenological perspective, the constructivist also rejects the idea that representativeness is a critical criterion in the selection process. Instead, she will typically work with a more pragmatic and loose criterion that suitable documents are texts that will be able to shed light on this issue in such a way that the final analysis generates new, convincing and interesting knowledge (Mik-Meyer & Justesen, 2010: 284f).

Villadsen (2006) argues—with reference to the work of Foucault—that the texts chosen for use in a constructivist analysis must be *exemplary* rather than representative. Exemplary texts are documents that illustrate a particular point in a particularly clear or interesting manner and demonstrate discursive rules or breaks within the field covered by the study. Often, it will also be particularly interesting to use documents that are reflective and clearly highlight a particular normative position (Villadsen, 2006: 101f). This is because the constructivist is often interested in studying how certain phenomena (for example "healthy employees," "good financial management" or "responsible management") are constructed in a particular way in a certain context. The assumption is that texts actively help shape the perception of what it means, for example, to be a responsible manager, and that the way a certain phenomenon is shaped is contingent (i.e., it could always have been different).

Some constructivist analyses have concentrated in particular on how documents help classify reality in a certain way (Bowker & Star, 2000). As we saw in the introductory chapter, this is related to the fact that the purpose of constructivist analyses is often to show that the categorisations of reality that we tend to take for granted and see as "natural" are contingent constructions that *could* have been different. It is in this light that several studies inspired by constructivism use documents from different periods to analyse and illustrate discursive changes over time.

Case study: Performance auditing

The case study we have chosen in order to shed light on document-analysis is based on a study by Justesen (2005; 2008) of the Danish National Audit Office's (NAO) performance audit practices. Justesen studied how NAO reports are compiled through a process that involves a number of different actors and institutional conditions (standards, legislation and other reports), which in different ways help to write and shape the text that ultimately appears as a single, official document. She also studied what happens with NAO reports when politicians and the media read, relay and *use* them in different ways.

The study adopted a constructivist perspective. Empirically, its starting point was a particular NAO performance audit of the Ministry of Foreign Affairs. This type of publication is publicly available, and the relevant documents were therefore downloaded from the NAO's own website. The key text in the study was the report on the Ministry's management of bilateral development aid. However, Justesen was also interested in how the documents were produced, and so applied for—and was granted—access to a wide range of material. The material included correspondence (emails, letters) between the NAO and the Ministry, a number of earlier drafts and the Ministry's highly comprehensive written responses to those drafts. Combined with interviews with officials from both the NAO and the Ministry, the author used this material to analyse how the report was the result of a collective, interactive and ambiguous writing process.

A focus of the study was also on *the consumption process*, with particular emphasis on how the published report was used and "translated" in new contexts. Here, Justesen referred, for example, to newspaper articles that cited the report. These documents were sourced via the Danish Infomedia database.

The following passages are brief extracts from the NAO report that formed the empirical starting point for the study. The original text amounts to a total of 73 pages:

"1. This report is addressed to the Public Accounts Committee pursuant to section 17 (2) of The Auditor General Act, cf. consolidated act no. 3, of 7 January 1997. The report deals with the Ministry's management of bilateral development aid.

[…]

3. The National Audit Office has ascertained that the Ministry of Foreign Affairs agrees that there is a need for effective and systematic target- and performance-management, cf. the report on the audit of the national budget for 1999 and Danida's annual report 2000.

4. The main purpose of this report is to examine whether the Ministry of Foreign Affairs applies target- and performance-management of bilateral aid efficiently. For illustrative and evaluative purposes, the National Audit Office has studied:

- whether the Ministry of Foreign Affairs has implemented the strategy by stipulating relevant operational and managerial targets,
- whether the Ministry of Foreign Affairs' management processes and internal follow-up support improvements to delivery, and
- whether the Ministry of Foreign Affairs' reporting contains a comprehensive account of activities and results.

[…]

38. A study of the material upon which the Ministry's management of the bilateral aid is based reveals that the Ministry of Foreign Affairs has only implemented the strategy to a very limited extent and has not stipulated operational performance targets. It is the view of the National Audit Office that setting pre-determined targets at all levels would improve the Ministry's ability to establish a direct link between strategy and action"

(Danish National Audit Office (Rigsrevisionen), 2002: 5f og 15).

Discussion of the case study

As previously mentioned, Justesen's study was based on a constructivist perspective, and this had a number of consequences in relation to both the selection process and the analysis of the documents included in the study. The choice of the performance audit report from which this extract was taken was based on a pragmatic evaluation that this document would serve to illustrate the problem. This was partly based on a preliminary search of Infomedia, which revealed that the report had generated considerable media coverage. This was significant because the study focused, among other things, on the consumption process.

The extent to which the report was particularly representative of NAO audits was thus less crucial, and the question of the report's "technical quality" was also completely subordinate. Intertextuality was a crucial principle in the selection of other documents. It quickly became apparent that the report related to many other texts in different ways. Firstly, it referred to a number of other documents. In the selected extract, we see, for example, that the report refers to legislation and to several of the Ministry's own documents. These documents therefore became part of Justesen's document material. The intertextuality aspect was crucial to the principle of involving earlier draft reports and the Ministry's responses. These texts were chosen to reflect the part of the problem that dealt with the production process for the report. In relation to the consumption process, too, intertextuality was crucial to the selection of relevant texts from the news coverage. Here, texts that referred directly to the relevant report were used.

In a realist perspective, the selection criteria would typically have been different. In the first instance, it would have been important to evaluate whether the selected text was representative of the NAO's work. Secondly, it would have been essential to evaluate the document's validity and reliability, and ask questions about the extent to which the reader could rely upon the report—i.e., to what degree does its content represent reality? Is the evidence contained in the report about the Ministry reliable? Is the NAO right or wrong when, as we see in the extract, it concludes that "the Ministry of Foreign Affairs has only implemented the strategy to a very limited extent"?

In a phenomenological perspective, the selection criteria would be more like those applied by the constructivist, even though there would possibly be a greater focus on the particular significance that the documents chosen had for the actors involved (for exsample the NAO and the Ministry). A text would be less relevant in this context if, for example through interviews, the initial phase of the study found that the report did not play a crucial role in the actors' understanding of their own everyday practice.

The analysis of the report would also look very different depending on whether it was based on a realist, phenomenological or constructivist perspective. In a realist-inspired perspective, a document such as a performance audit could be read as more or less qualified evidence of how the Ministry *is* actually run. If the document was evaluated as being valid and reliable, it would be possible for the reader to use it as a kind of window into the reality of the Ministry's management, which was the topic of the report.

In the realist-based analysis, the student will often relate reflexively to the document by triangulating with other sources or methods, in order to ensure that the source actually does reflect the conditions that the study wishes to elucidate. If other sources "say the same" as the report, it will increase the credibility of the analysis. To the extent that there is any focus on the importance of context for the production of the report, this will be in relation to evaluating possible bias that might reduce the report's validity and reliability. In this sense, good material consists of documents that are not *biased* but seek objectivity, as it is precisely this type of document that is expected to shed light on actual aspects of reality.

The phenomenologist will approach the analysis of a document like the one cited above quite differently. She might look at the motivation behind the production of the report. The student will typically combine document analysis with qualitative personal interviews with the report's authors. The focus is therefore on the production, but instead of focusing on intertextuality—as in a constructivist analysis—the phenomenology-inspired student will typically be interested in the subjective motives for producing the report. Another possibility within the phenomenology perspective would be to focus on the consumption process. Here, too, it would be an obvious choice to use interviews to identify the impact of a document in relation to the actors' life-worlds. For example, many organisations have formulated a set of basic values, but what is important in this perspective is not the content of those values but how they are interpreted by subjective actors. If nobody in the organisation knows about a document, or what it actually says, then it is considered to be uninteresting. In other words, the document is assumed not to have an inherent significance; rather, it is only meaningful to the extent that it is interpreted, understood and related to subjective provinces of meaning (Schutz & Natanson, 1962).

The document material is not assumed to have an inherent and stable meaning either, so context is always crucial in a constructivist analysis. Context plays a role in the production, appearance and consumption of a document. The analysis will often focus on interactive, contingent processes, the aim of which is to make it clear that meaning is generated in a manner that could always have been different. As an extension of this, constructivist analyses often also focus on how the text helps to create a certain picture of reality. The interesting thing in the constructivist analysis is not whether this picture is "true" in a correspondence-theory sense, but rather *how* the text presents certain conditions as factual, objective or indubitable (Mik-Meyer, 2005). In relation to the extract from the report, it is interesting to analyse rhetorical strategies, for example. It is notable that the author's position is obscured by phrases such as "the study has shown" and, in general, the presentation is in language that signals objectivity (Justesen & Skærbæk, 2005).

Summary

In this chapter, we have discussed how documents are a particular form of qualitative material that requires methodological reflection to the same degree as interviews, participant observation or focus groups. On the one hand, documents are data produced independently of the student's study and how she designs it. On the other hand, it is important to reflect on how this material will assume special meaning in relation to the problem.

As in the other chapters, we have argued that both the perception of what kind of material the documents are and the practicalities of document studies are closely linked to the theoretical perspective. By way of a summary, we can say that, in the realist perspective, documents will be seen as sources that ideally tell students about objective factors *outside* of the text. Ideally, the document is a witness to, or a window upon, reality. In the phenomenology perspective, parentheses are placed around the question of whether the contents reflect objective, factual circumstances in reality. Here, what is interesting is how the document relates to the subjective world. The analysis will therefore focus on motives (why did the people who wrote the document do so?) and interpretations (how do the document's readers interpret the text, and how will it be meaningful in relation to their subjective universe of meaning?). In a constructivist perspective, it is not important whether the documents say something "true" about conditions in reality. Instead, it is the text's relation to its context that is interesting. The idea of context is understood here more widely than in the phenomenological perspective, and consists not only of individual actors but also, for example, discourses and institutional conditions.

Suggested reading
Paul Atkinson and Amanda Coffey's (2004) article "Analysing Documentary Realities" discusses how documents play an important role in contemporary organisations, and how we can analyse them.

Lindsay Prior's *Using Documents in Social Research* (2003) gives a thorough introduction to document analysis. The book holds many other good references to research that uses documents (and reflects upon this particular method).

Exercises

1) Discuss different types of selection criteria for document studies.

2) Formulate a research question in which it is important that the selected documents are representative, and another in which this criterion is not so crucial.

3) Discuss how the relationship between the document and reality is viewed in the three perspectives. What are the main differences between the perspectives? And where is there overlap?

4) Formulate a research question that focuses on how documents are used and interpreted in an everyday organisational context.

5) Discuss how you, via your own study design, affect the reading of the document material.

Qualitative research methods in organisation studies

Introduction

In this book we have argued that it is important for students to be well prepared when embarking on a study that is based on qualitative methods and therefore bases its analysis on qualitative empirical material. Being well prepared is about more than just practical considerations regarding things like the choice of interviewee or the focus points in participant observation.

At the most basic level, being well prepared is about the student being able to justify and defend the range of choices she has to make when she chooses to use qualitative methods. It is therefore about both the choice of theoretical perspective—which in this book we have illustrated with realism, phenomenology and constructivism—and the series of choices linked to the specific methods used to collect the data or produce the empirical material "required" to address the problem.

Research question, theory and method

Formulating a research question is central to all of these choices. A good research question is crucial for a qualitative study. By a "good" research question, we mean one that is practical—i.e., it poses questions that it is possible to answer in the (typically short) time students have in which to prepare their projects. We also mean one that is framed in a way that corresponds with the perspective in which the student has a particular interest. Coherence and consistency are important criteria for a successful project—i.e., the individual parts of the study must be coherent and its concepts, methodology and theories applied in a consistent manner.

It might be said, *inter alia*, that the research question, choice of theory and choice of methods are inextricably linked, which means that if you adjust the research question, change your perspective or suddenly decide, for example, to drop participant observation in favour of interviews, this will have an impact on all three parts, not just the individual component you are changing. Let us look at an example of how the three elements are linked, based on a hypothetical situation in which the student decides to change her research question. As we have addressed previously in this book, there is a great deal of difference between the type of knowledge that you can attain by using "how" and "why" research questions. In brief (and somewhat bluntly), "how" questions lead to project descriptions that focus on context, while "why" questions typically seek to identify general causal patterns that apply to more than just a specific context. In terms of methodology and theory, it is important, therefore, whether the student chooses a formulation designed to shed light on the causality associated with the study of a phenomenon or, conversely, whether the formulation is designed to shed light on the processes associated with the study of a phenomenon. In the former case, realism would seem to be the most obvious perspective. In the latter, the constructivist or phenomenological perspective would typically be the most obvious. Further, in relation to the choice of methods, a "why" problem would be best answered by the use of a structured interview guide or structured observation, while a "how" problem is most likely to be answered by the use of a more exploratory approach involving less structured interviews, focus groups, document studies or participant observations.

Students often ask in what order they should make these decisions. Should we always start with formulating the research question, then choose the perspective that reflects it and finally decide on which methodology to apply? Or should we do it the other way around? As we have pointed out several times in the previous chapters, most answers to questions concerning the specific choices that students have to make when preparing a qualitative project relate to the specific situation. However, there is still a rule of thumb that can be applied.

In many cases, a qualitative study will arise out of curiosity: there is something you do not understand and would like to explore, either in the form of an explanation of causal relations (realism) or by approaching an understanding of the phenomenon (constructivism/phenomenology). Regardless of perspective, your curiosity is translated into a research problem. The actual work of formulating the research question then begins: you draw up draft formulations, which pave the way for an analysis that provides the desired explanation/understanding of the phenomenon. You then consider which theories/concepts it would be useful to incorporate into the study and think about the choice of data material—and, therefore, methodology. The more specific you are in these reflections, the better equipped you will be to identify whether your research question is too broad, too vague or perhaps too ambitious.

In the realism-informed project, research questions often end with the student developing the hypotheses that the study is designed to test (and possibly verify or falsify). In the constructivism- and/or phenomenology-inspired project, formulating the research question is a process that, in principle, does not stop until the student presses the print button and submits her assignment.

Choice of qualitative method

If, as we have done in this book, we look in detail at the many reflections linked to the choice of methods and practical approaches, it becomes apparent that the process is both time-consuming and challenging. Let us consider an example.

Two students have fine-tuned their question in relation to the choice of perspective, theories and methods. They have decided to use the interview as the primary method of obtaining knowledge about the phenomenon that is the focus of their study. In addition to thinking about who they want to interview, where the interview will take place, and how it will be documented and subsequently analysed, they must also think about a series of technical aspects of the interview procedure. Will they work with a structured, semi-structured or unstructured interview guide? How will the degree of structuring be linked to the perspective on which the study is based? Will their questions be obvious and relevant to their interviewees, or should they start with a pilot test of the interview guide? And then: how will they guarantee the interviewees' anonymity, not only in relation to the public but also inside the organisation (which, of course, is aware of the study and will be allowed to read the results afterward)? Is the subject matter so "sensitive" that they should mark the study as confidential, or is this unnecessary? And so on, and so on.

We have focused on questions like these in the four chapters on interviews, focus groups, participant observation and document studies. It has not been our intention to put students off and cause them to lose confidence in their ability to conduct a qualitative study. Rather, the sole purpose has been to present theoretically based practical discussions of the four data collection methods in order to provide students with the requisite knowledge for a good qualitative project.

These four chapters also looked at cases from the following

areas of organisation studies: human resource management (the interview chapter), marketing (the focus-group chapter), corporate social responsibility (the participant-observation chapter) and performance auditing (the document-studies chapter). Cases from organisation studies were chosen to make our discussions of methodology as practical and tangible as possible. We wanted the discussions to be practical both in relation to the typical problems faced when using qualitative methods and in relation to obvious themes for organisation studies students. These four chapters also relate our discussions of methodology to the three perspectives—realism, phenomenology and constructivism—presented in the first two chapters. These three perspectives form the basis for reflection in all of the discussions throughout the book.

Choice of perspective: realism, phenomenology or constructivism?

As we mentioned in Chapter One, there are an almost infinite number of ways in which to present and delineate the different perspectives—sometimes known as "paradigms"—on which a qualitative study can be based. We have chosen the perspectives of realism, phenomenology and constructivism precisely because these are frequently used in organisational research. As stated several times in the book, there are, of course, other ways to describe and delineate the perspectives on the social world that researchers study. Our choice to highlight these three perspectives was a pragmatic one, as they are the ones commonly adopted by students in organisation studies.

The book's four chapters on specific qualitative methods (3–6) all draw on our introductory presentation and discussion of these three perspectives, so we strongly recommend that students read Chapter One first. In it, we also introduce and discuss the concepts of ontology and epistemology, since they reflect two important aspects of any social research study—namely, how we see the nature of the world (ontology) and how we acquire knowledge of this nature (epistemology). If you work with theoretical-informed questions or perspectives, you will therefore necessarily distinguish between theories precisely on the basis of their ontological and epistemological view. In other words, these two concepts focus sharply on the fundamental differences that may exist in terms of understanding the reality that surrounds us and of which we are part, and therefore also on how we can acquire knowledge of this reality.

To summarise our discussions of the three different perspectives, it might be said that the realist perspective assumes that there is a single reality that exists in a particular way, regardless of our knowledge of it and the language we use to describe it. The phenomenological perspective assumes that there are several different realities, since reality as a concept is only interesting and meaningful if we understand it in terms of the subjects' experience and interpretations. The constructivist perspective goes a little further, and assumes that our understanding of reality is a social and linguistic construction (hence "constructivism") and therefore reality does not have any form of inherent essence. However, even this does not mean that the concept of reality is abandoned. Instead, it is merely stressed that reality has been and continues to be constructed via contingent social processes, and that it could therefore always have looked different.

At first glance, you might think that all these discussions are not relevant to conducting analyses of organisations. In other words, why is it necessary to take an interest in ontology, epistemology and perspectives when you just have to study, for example, how or why organisations work with corporate social responsibility? Our discussions in Chapter One—and, in fact, in all the other chapters—will hopefully have countered this kind of objection. In other words, we hope that the discussions in this book have convinced the critical student of why this type of knowledge is a prerequisite for a successful qualitative research project. We do not have the space here to refer to the many discussions in detail, but it is worth reiterating one important reason for taking theoretical and methodological reflections seriously.

The academic world is concerned with producing knowledge that differs from fiction because it relates to research practices and communities that are always concerned with discussing what is true, good, necessary and interesting. In other words, in any area of study, the research community is aware of the power that various studies possess. We are all familiar with the role of "the expert" in the media: if an expert thinks this or that, then it must be true, because experts' arguments are afforded greater weight precisely because of their expertise. Experts' arguments are certainly weighed more heavily than those of laymen. But what is expertise if it does not reflect a consensus in a research community on how best to examine a phenomenon and subsequently comment on it?

In the academic world, which is society's major producer of experts and expertise, quality is dependent upon a researcher following a series of rules on how to approach studies, what reflections and considerations should be made, how the material is subsequently processed and what publication strategy is used. In other words, a study's findings can be all very interesting but the key is the assumption that this knowledge is of a particularly high quality, and therefore possesses a particular validity. We have therefore also included a chapter (Chapter Two) on quality criteria in qualitative research.

Quality criteria

As we argue in Chapter Two, it is crucial to reflect on and apply quality criteria—i.e., the parameters for evaluation that researchers and students use in their efforts to produce good research, and to which both groups look when reading other people's studies—throughout the study process. Quality criteria set out the evaluation categories that ensure research is of high quality and has a particularly high level of credibility. There is consensus on this issue across the three perspectives. Although there are some differences about which criteria should be weighted, nobody suggests that the question of research quality is a purely subjective matter. For some, it is essential to design a study that, in principle, can be reproduced quite accurately by others and whose findings can be generalised (realism). For others, it is first and foremost about being able to demonstrate quality in craftsmanship (phenomenology). Finally, there are those who stress more pragmatic criteria, such as being convincing and producing relevant knowledge (constructivism).

In Chapter Two, therefore, we present both criteria that relate to all qualitative social research and criteria that relate specifically to each of the three perspectives. Just as it is sensible for a student to read the curriculum before sitting for an exam, in order to be aware of what she is expected to have learned and on which she will therefore be examined, it is also sensible to reflect on the criteria for "good research" upon which we would wish our project to be evaluated. We therefore also argue that students should start to think about quality criteria in the very beginning of project work. The choice of quality criteria has a number of practical consequences for the work.

Reflecting on quality criteria helps to improve the quality of studies produced by both researchers and students. Pragmatically, it might also be said that if a student chooses not to consider or explicate what she has done to ensure the quality of a project she submits as part of an examination, then the internal or external examiners will lack a crucial element needed in order to assess the quality of the project. We therefore emphasise the importance of the transparency criterion, which stresses that all methodical and theoretical choices and approaches must be *explicitly* described and justified, regardless of the perspective with which we choose to work.

Summary

We are aware that a wide range of textbooks on qualitative methods already exists, and we have, of course, had to delineate our project—this book—in relation to this existing literature. We believe that this particular book differs from most others in a number of areas that make it particularly relevant for students of organisational research:

1) It anchors qualitative methods in three frequently used perspectives in organisational research (realism, phenomenology and constructivism);
2) It alternates between discussions of theory and highly practical considerations of how to conduct qualitative research;
3) It presents the four most frequently used qualitative data collection methods in organisational research (interviews, focus groups, participant observation and document studies);
4) It relates these methods to four areas of study for organisational research (human resource management (HRM), marketing, CSR and performance auditing).

Bibliography

Alvesson, M. (1998): "Gender Relations and Identity at Work: A case study of masculinities and femininities at an advertising agency," *Human Relations*, 51(8): 969–1005.

Alvesson, M. & Sköldberg, K. (2000): *Reflexive Methodology. New vistas for qualitative research.* London: Sage.

Atkinson, P. & Coffey, A. (2004): "Analysing Documentary Realities," in D. Silverman (ed.): *Qualitative Research: Theory, method, practice.* London: Sage.

Bakhtin, M.M. (1986): "The Problem of Speech Genres," in M. Bakhtin (ed.): *Speech Genres & Other Essays.* Austin: University of Texas Press.

Berger, P. & Luckmann, T. (1991): *The Social Construction of Reality.* London: Penguin Books.

Bloor, M., Frankland, J., Thomas, M. & Robson, K. (2001): *Focus Groups in Social Research.* London: Sage.

Booth, W.C., Colomb, G.G. & Williams, J.M. (2003): *The Craft of Research*, 2nd edition. Chicago & London: The University of Chicago Press.

Bowker, G.G. & Star, S.L. (2000): *Sorting Things Out: Classification and its consequences.* Cambridge, MA: MIT Press.

Burr, V. (1998): "Overview: Realism, relativism, social constructionism and discourse," in I. Parker (ed.): *Social Constructionism, Discourse and Realism.* London: Sage.

Carrigan, M. & Attalla, A. (2001): "The Myth of the Ethical Consumer: Do ethics matter in purchase behavior?" *Journal of Consumer Marketing*, 18(7): 560–577.

Collin, F. (1998): "Socialkonstruktivisme og den Sociale Virkelighed (Social Constructivism and Social Reality)," in M. Järvinen & M. Bertilsson (eds.): *Socialkonstruktivisme. Bidrag til en kritisk diskussion (Social Constructivism: Contribution to a critical discussion).* Copenhagen: Hans Reitzels Forlag.

Collin, F. (2003): *Konstruktivisme (Constructivism)*. Frederiksberg: Sam-fundslitteratur & Roskilde Universitetsforlag.

Cooren, F. (2004): "Textual Agency: How texts do things in organizational settings," *Organization*, 11(3): 373–393.

Croll, P. (1986): *Systematic Classroom Observation*. London: Falmer.

Czarniawska-Joerges, B. (1992): "Budgets as Texts: On collective writing in the public sector," *Accounting, Management & Information Technologies*, 2(4): 221–239.

Danish National Audit Office (Rigsrevisionen) (2002): *Beretning om Udenrigsministeriets styring af den bilaterale udviklingsbistand. Statsrevisorernes beretning nr. 5/01 (Report on How the Ministry of Foreign Affairs Manages Bilateral Development Aid: The National Audit Office report no. 5/01)*. Copenhagen.

Davison, J. (2007): "Photographs and Accountability: Cracking the code of an NGO," *Accounting, Auditing & Accountability Journal*, 20(1): 133–158.

Demant, J. (2006): "Fokusgruppen—Spørgsmål til fænomener i nuet (The Focus Group: Questions about phenomena in the present)," in O. Bjerg & K. Villadsen (eds.): *Sociologiske Metoder—Fra teori til analyse i kvantitative og kvalitative studier (Sociological Methodology: From theory to analysis in quantitative and qualitative studies)*. Frederiksberg: Samfundslitteratur.

Denscombe, M. (2007): *The Good Research Guide for Small-scale Social Research Projects*. Berkshire: Open University Press.

Denzin, N.K. & Lincoln, Y.S. (2000): "Introduction: The discipline and practice of qualitative research," in N.K. Denzin & Y.S. Lincoln (eds.): *Handbook of Qualitative Research*, 2nd edition. London: Sage.

Ellis, C. & Berger, L. (2002): "Their Story/My Story/Our Story: Including the researcher's experience in interview research," in J.F. Gubrium & J.A. Holstein (eds.): *Handbook of Interview Research: Context and method*. London: Sage Publications.

Emerson, R., Fretz, R. & Shaw, L. (1995): *Writing Ethnographic Fieldnotes*. Chicago: University of Chicago Press.

Eriksson, P. & Kovalainen, A. (2008): *Qualitative Methods in Business Research*. London: Sage.

Esterberg, K.G. (2002): *Qualitative Methods in Social Research*. Boston: McGraw-Hill.

Fontana, A. & Frey, J.H. (2002): "Interviewing: The art of science," in N.K. Denzin & Y.S. Lincoln (eds.): *Handbook of Qualitative Research,* 2nd edition. London: Sage.

Geertz, C. (1973): *The Interpretations of Cultures. Selected essays.* New York: Basic Books.

Gergen, M.M. & Gergen, K.J. (2002): "Qualitative Inquiry: Tensions and transformations," in N.K. Denzin & Y.S. Lincoln (eds.): *Handbook of Qualitative Research,* 2nd edition. London: Sage.

Gheradi, S. & Nicolini, D. (2002): "Learning the Trade: A culture of safety in practice," *Organization,* 9(2): 191–223.

Gillham, B. (2005): *Research Interviewing: The range of techniques.* Berkshire: Open University Press.

Giorgi, A. (1997): "The Theory, Practice, and Evaluation of the Phenomenological Method as a Qualitative Research Procedure," *Journal of Phenomenological Psychology,* 27(2): 235–261.

Goffman, E. (1959): *The Presentation of Self in Everyday Life.* London: Penguin Books.

Goffman, E. (1961): *Asylums: Essays on the social situation of mental patients and other inmates.* New York: Anchor Books.

Gold, R. (1969): "Roles in Sociological Field Observation," in G. McCall & J. Simmons (eds.): *Issues in Participant Observation: A text and reader.* London: Addison Wesley.

Gubrium, J.F. & Holstein, J.A. (2002): "From the Individual Interview to the Interview Society," in J.F. Gubrium & J.A. Holstein (eds.): *Handbook of Interview Research: Context and method.* London: Sage.

Halkier, B. (2002): *Fokusgrupper (Focus Groups).* Frederiksberg: Samfundslitteratur & Roskilde Universitetsforlag.

Hammersley, M. & Atkinson, P. (2002): *Ethnography: Principles in practice.* London: Routledge.

Harper, D. (2002): "Reimagining Visual Methods: Galileo to Neuromancer," in N.K. Denzin & Y. S. Lincoln (eds.): *Handbook of Qualitative Research,* 2nd edition. London: Sage.

Hazen, M.A. (1993): "Towards Polyphonic Organization," *Journal of Organizational Change Management,* 6(5): 15–26.

Hedland, T.N. (1990): "Chapter 1: Introduction," in T.N. Hedland, K.L. Pike & M. Harris (eds.): *Emics and Etics: The insider/outsider debate.* London: Sage.

Holstein, J.A. & Gubrium, J.F. (1995): *The Active Interview*. Thousand Oaks, CA: Sage.

Holstein, J.A. & Gubrium, J.F. (2004): "The Active Interview," in D. Silverman (ed.): *Qualitative Research: Theory, method and practice*. London: Sage.

Järvinen, M. (2001): "Accounting for Trouble: Identity negotiations in qualitative interviews with alcoholics," *Symbolic Interaction*, 24(3): 263–284.

Järvinen, M. & Mik-Meyer, N. (2005): "Observationer i en Interaktionistisk Begrebsramme (Observations in an Interactionist Perspective)," in M. Järvinen & N. Mik-Meyer (eds.): *Kvalitative Metoder i et Interaktionistisk Perspektiv (Qualitative Methods in an Interactionist Perspective)*. Copenhagen: Hans Reitzels Forlag.

Jespersen, J. (2004): "Kritisk Realisme—Teori og praksis (Critical Realism: Theory and practice)," in L. Fuglsang & P. Bitsch Olsen (eds.): *Videnskabsteori i Samfundsvidenskaberne: På tværs af fagkulturer og paradigmer (Science Theory in the Social Sciences: Transcending subject cultures and paradigms)*, 2nd edition. Frederiksberg: Roskilde Universitetsforlag.

Justesen, L. (2005): "Dokumenter i Netværk (Documents in Networks)," in M. Järvinen & N. Mik-Meyer (eds.): *Kvalitative Metoder i et Interaktionistisk Perspektiv (Qualitative Methods in an Interactionist Perspective)*. Copenhagen: Hans Reitzels Forlag.

Justesen, L. (2008): *Kunsten at Skrive Revisionsrapporter. En beretning om forvaltningsrevisionens beretninger (The Art of Writing Audit Reports: A report about reports by auditors)*, PhD thesis, Copenhagen Business School.

Justesen, L. & Skærbæk, P. (2005): "Performance Auditing and the Production of Discomfort," in S. Jönsson & J. Mouritsen (eds.): *Accounting in Scandinavia: The Northern Lights*. Kristiansstad: Liber & Copenhagen Business School Press.

Kirk, J. & Miller, M.L. (1986): *Reliability and Validity in Qualitative Research*. Thousand Oaks, CA: Sage.

Kunda, G. (1992): *Engineering Culture: Control and commitment in a high-tech corporation*. Philadelphia, PA: Temple University Press.

Kvale, S. (1996): *InterViews. An introduction to qualitative research interviewing*. Thousand Oaks, CA: Sage.

Latour, B. (1987): *Science in Action*. Cambridge, MA: Harvard University Press.

Lawson, T. (1997): *Economics and Reality*. London: Routledge.

Lezaun, J. (2007): "A Market of Opinions: The political epistemology of focus groups," in M. Callon, Y. Millo & F. Muniesa (eds.): *Market Devices*. Oxford: Blackwell Publishing/The Sociological Review.

Llewellyn, N. & Harrison, A. (2006): "Resisting Corporate Communications: Insights into folk linguistics," *Human Relations*, 59(4): 567–596.

Lowndes, S. (2005): "The E-mail Interview," in B. Gillham (ed.): *Research Interviewing: The range of techniques*. Berkshire: Open University Press.

May, T. (2001): *Social Research: Issues, methods and processes*, 3rd edition. Maidenhead: Open University Press.

Merton, R.K. (1987): "Focused Interview and Focus Groups: Continuities and discontinuities," *Public Opinion Quarterly*, 51: 550–557.

Merton, R.K. & Kendall, P.L. (1946): "The Focused Interview," *The American Journal of Sociology*, 51(6): 541–557.

Meyer, J.W. & Rowan, B. (1977): "Institutional Organizations: Formal structure as myth and ceremony," *The American Journal of Sociology*, 83(2): 340–363.

Mik-Meyer, N. (2005): "Dokumenter i en Interaktionistisk Begrebsramme (Documents in an Interactionist Conceptual Framework)," in M. Järvinen & N. Mik-Meyer (eds.): *Kvalitative Metoder i et Interaktionistisk Perspektiv (Qualitative Methods in an Interactionist Perspective)*. Copenhagen: Hans Reitzels Forlag.

Mik-Meyer, N. (2009): "Managing Fat Bodies: Identity regulation between public and private domains," *Critical Social Studies*, 10(2): 20–35.

Mik-Meyer, N. (2010): "Metodekombination (Combining Methods)," in P. Darmer, B. Jordansen, J. Astrup Madsen & J. Thomsen (eds.): *Paradigmer i Praksis: Anvendelse af metoder til studier af organiserings- og ledelsesprocesser (Paradigms in Practice: Use of methodology in the study of organisational and management processes)*. Frederiksberg: Handelshøjskolens Forlag.

Mik-Meyer, N. & Justesen, L. (2010): "Dokumentanalyse (Document Analysis)," in P. Darmer, B. Jordansen, J. Astrup Madsen & J. Thomsen (eds.): *Paradigmer i Praksis: Anvendelse af metoder til studier af organiserings- og ledelsesprocesser (Paradigms in Practice: Use of methodology in the study of organisational and management processes).* Frederiksberg: Handelshøjskolens Forlag.

Mik-Meyer, N. & Villadsen, K. (2012): *Power, Citizenship and Social Welfare: Human service encounters between the citizen and the state.* London: Routledge (forthcoming).

Morgan, D. (1996): "Focus Groups," *Annual Review of Sociology,* 22: 129–152.

Myers, M.D. (2009): *Qualitative Research in Business and Management.* London: Sage.

Patton, M.Q. (1990): *Qualitative Evaluation and Research Methods,* 2nd edition. Thousand Oaks, CA: Sage.

Peräkylä, A. (2003): "Reliability and Validity in Research on Naturally Occurring Social Interaction," in D. Silverman (ed.): *Qualitative Analysis: Issues of theory and method.* London: Sage.

Pietras-Jensen, V. (2007a): "At Læse Finansielle Regnskaber (Reading Financial Accounts)," in L. Fuglsang, P. Hagedorn-Rasmussen & P. Bitsch Olsen (eds.): *Teknikker i Samfundsvidenskaberne (Techniques in the Social Sciences).* Frederiksberg: Roskilde Universitetsforlag.

Pietras-Jensen, V. (2007b): "At Læse Ikke-finansielle Regnskaber (Reading Non-financial Accounts)," in L. Fuglsang, P. Hagedorn-Rasmussen & P. Bitsch Olsen (eds.): *Teknikker i Samfundsvidenskaberne (Techniques in the Social Sciences).* Frederiksberg: Roskilde Universitetsforlag.

Polanyi, M. (1966): *The Tacit Dimension.* London: Routledge & Kegan Paul.

Power, M. (1997): *The Audit Society.* Oxford: Oxford University Press.

Prior, L. (2003): *Using Documents in Social Research.* London: Sage.

Riessman, C.K. (1993): *Narrative Analysis.* Newbury Park, CA: Sage.

Roepstorff, A.K. (2010): *CSR—Virksomheders sociale ansvar som begreb og praksis (Corporate Social Responsibility as a Concept and in Practice).* Copenhagen: Hans Reitzels Forlag.

Schutz, A. (1970): *On Phenomenology and Social Relations.* Chicago: University of Chicago Press.

Schutz, A. & Natanson, M. (1962): *Collected Papers: The problem of social reality.* The Hague: M. Nijhoff.

Silverman, D. (2001): *Interpreting Qualitative Data: Methods for analysing talk, text and interaction.* London: Sage.

Simon, A. & Boyer, G. (1970): *Mirrors of Behavior: An anthology of classroom observation instruments.* Philadelphia: Research for Better Schools.

Singleton, R.A. & Straits, B.C. (2002): "Survey Interviewing," in J.F. Gubrium & J.A. Holstein (eds.): *Handbook of Interview Research.* Thousand Oaks, CA: Sage.

Søndergaard, D.M. (2002): "Poststructuralist Approaches to Empirical Analysis," *International Journal of Qualitative Studies in Education,* 15(2): 187–204.

Staunæs, D. & Søndergaard, D.M. (2008): *Høns i Hanegården. Køn og ledelse (Chickens in the Rooster's Den: Gender and management).* Copenhagen: Danish School of Education.

Stewart, D.W., Shamdasani, P.N. & Rook, D.W. (2007): *Focus Groups: Theory and practice.* Thousand Oaks, CA: Sage.

Van Maanen, J. & Pentland, B.T. (1994): "Cops and Auditors: The rhetoric of records," in S.B. Sithkin & R.J. Bies (eds.): *The Legalistic Organization.* Thousand Oaks, CA: Sage.

Villadsen, K. (2006): "Genealogi som Metode—Fornuftens tilblivelseshistorier (Genealogy as a Method: The becoming of rationality)," in O. Bjerg & K. Villadsen (eds.): *Sociologiske Metoder—Fra teori til analyse i kvantitative og kvalitative studier (Sociological Methods: From theory to analysis in quantitative and qualitative studies).* Frederiksberg: Samfundslitteratur.

Watson, T. (1994): *In Search of Management: Culture, chaos and control in managerial work.* London: Routledge.

Weber, M. (2005): "Bureaucracy," in J.M. Shafritz, J. Steven Ott & Y. Suk Jang, *Classics of Organisational Theory.* Belmont, CA: Wadsworth.

Wolcott, H. (1995): *The Art of Fieldwork.* Oxford: AltaMira Press.

Ybema, S., Yanov, S., Wels, H. & Kamsteeg, F.H. (2009): *Organizational Ethnography: Studying the complexity of everyday life.* London: Sage.

Yin, R.K. (2003): *Case Study Research: Design and methods,* 3rd edition. London: Sage.

Biographies

Lise Justesen has a Masters in Philosophy from the University of Copenhagen and has a PhD from Copenhagen Business School. She is an associate professor in the Department of Organisation, Copenhagen Business School. Her published works include several articles on qualitative methods.

Nanna Mik-Meyer has a Masters in Anthropology and a PhD in Sociology from the University of Copenhagen. She is an associate professor in the Department of Organisation, Copenhagen Business School. Her published works include a number of books and articles on qualitative methodology and the meeting between citizen and state. See www.mik-meyer.com